To Kevin,

Look forward to comments &
helping your customers

What executives are saying about Gary Patterson:

"The FiscalDoctor's sound marketing advice, incisive insights, and best practices are recession-proof. Stop worrying about the economy and start implementing these practices today. Your company will grow stronger for it."

Dan Janal, author "Reporters are Looking for YOU!" and Founder of PRLEADS.com

*"Tired of treading water? Grab hold of **Million Dollar Blind Spots.** By applying these best practices, you'll shift your company out of fear and paralysis and into momentum and accelerated results. Prosperity is right in front of you. Learn where to look."*

Pegine Echevarria, CSP, MSW speaker, author and President of Team Pegine Inc named SBA's Women in Business Champion for Florida & NFL Minority Enterprise Development Week Entrepreneur of the Year

"The FiscalDoctor's insights, advice and best practices, while not primarily aimed at nonprofit, nonetheless empower nonprofit leaders to drag hidden needs and opportunities out of the darkness, and into meetings where they can be discussed and solved."

Karen Eber Davis, strategic consultant Contributor to Advancing the Non Profit Sector

"From first aid to internal medicine to physical therapy, the Fiscal Doctor knows what ails you. This book provides you and your business with proven, powerful fundamentals: hard-core numbers your company needs to put pressure on the wound, cure the infection, and build back speed and stamina for a lifetime of healthy profitability."

Diane Bogino
President, Performance Strategies, Inc.

"This is your road map, this is your game plan. This is the good stuff, and it will teach you 500 things about being more effective, more profitable and more empowered on the job."

Adam Haverson, CPA, CFA
CapTech Consulting

"Great leaders ask great questions. This book is your guide to asking them."

Gene Griessman, Ph.D.
Author, The Words Lincoln Lived By

"No matter the size of the company you lead, this practical and resourceful book will help you turn your business strategies into high-performance results."

David Roache
Managing Partner, connectC

"Knowing what you don't know is more important than what you do. Gary helps you look around all the clutter of the trees so you can see where your forest is burning."

Mitchell Davis
Editor - Yearbook of Experts(R)

"Eye-opening, incisive and thoughtful. One of the best business books I have read and I advise all venture capitalists to read it before serving on boards."

Tan Yinglan
author of Chinnovation, The Way of the VC & New Venture Creation

"Your value from Gary Patterson, in his books and consulting, is that he spares you reams of theory, and lasers in on practical, powerful and proven applications. In every situation, he banks on real-world facts and figures, and is generous with his knowledge, experience and money-making expertise."

Dick Dauphinais
President, Virtual Human Resource

"If you're tired of treading water, grab hold of Your Million Dollar Blind Spots. In applying these best practices, you'll shift your company out of the cold depths and into exciting, active, growth potential."

Elyse R. Greenbaum
Founder, ERG Consulting

Many Thanks...

With heartfelt gratitude to the following, for their time, talent and valuable perspective toward the completion of this book, I thank, in alphabetical order:

Scott Anderson, Paige Arnof-Fenn, Dave Butler, John Chapin, Mary Cole, Dick Dauphinais, Mitch Davis, Julia B. Ellingboe, Bonni DiMatteo, Pegine Echevarria, James Gilreath, Ellen Bohn Gitlitz, Hugh Glazer, Elyse Greenbaum, Larry Grumer, Linda Henman,Randy Houk, Bob Katz, Richard Kirby, Alexandra Lajoux, Duncan Martin, Bonnie Mattick, Roberta Matuson, Jim O'Donnell, Margaret Orem, Christen Patterson, Gary Patterson Jr., Kathy Patterson, Andy Peck, Matt Podowitz, Charlie Ricker, Gary Rush, Don Saracen, Roy Sequeira, John Snyder, Carol Stewart, Yinglan Tan, Dan Towle, Denise Williams, Rick Williams, and Bob Williamson.

This was my team.

Million Dollar Blind Spots

20/20 Vision for Financial Growth

Gary W. Patterson

The FiscalDoctor®

AudioInk Publishers
Issaquah
A Division of Made For Success, Inc.
www.AudioInk.com

Library of Congress Cataloging-in-Publication Data

Patterson, Gary W.
    Million-dollar blind spots : 20/20 vision for financial growth / Gary
    Patterson.
        p. cm.
        ISBN: 9780982241578 (alk. paper)

LC control no.: 2012943081LCCN

Distributed by AudioInk – www.AudioInk.com

For further information contact AudioInk Publishing, 1-425-526-6480

Table of Contents

"Good judgment is the result of experience, and experience the result of bad judgment."

— *Mark Twain*

Introduction

Too many executives suffer a sort of self-inflicted myopia. While they look busy enough with their head lowered to our day-to-day tasks, they fail to look around—and note solvable problems that keep the team from meeting its long-range business objectives.

Simply put, our teammates probably aren't telling us what we need to know, and we may not be providing as much value as we're capable of providing. This book will help you to understand the difference between your organization's deep-rooted problems that never seem to get resolved, and the symptoms that sometimes get treated, but are usually ignored until it's too late—if not for the organization, then certainly for someone's reputation or career.

I speak from personal experience that goes back more than 20 years, and starts with a defining moment as the new chief financial officer of a company that I was hired to help take through a lucrative sale, probably as an IPO. This was a career-launching move with a huge anticipated payday for me at a $40 million enterprise, whose innovative business had grown so consistently that the *Inc. 500* honored it three years running as a top-growth company. Yet at my second week on the job, I discovered that we had placed $30 million worth of purchase orders for product—suitcases—that nobody recalled placing. Even if we had wanted them, they were the wrong models, and we couldn't begin to store the massive volume. Have you ever been stuck with $100 million of suitcases at retail? Neither had I.

How would you survive this liquidity crisis? How would you protect your CEO, who had personally guaranteed the order, and spare him and all of his officers from public humiliation? How would you save a company's worth of jobs and growth potential? How would I? We faced ruin.

We regrouped. I led an investigation and tracked down the problem (the details are confidential). The company followed my action plan to the T: it obtained a $25 million bank line, met its obligations, and lived to fight another day. The company is still selling suitcases today. It's still an industry leader, still a household name, still synonymous with quality, reliability, and going places.

The experience I gained from solving that multi-million-dollar blind spot—and many others—prepared me for a career as a successful and highly sought-after consultant who delivers, in effect, *enterprise risk management on steroids*. As a frequent speaker and consultant on leadership, cooperation, communication, and risk, and as a business veteran who has led every functional department in this book, I've helped companies for more than thirty years locate more than an estimated $100 million of benefits, combined.

I wanted to help others avoid making the obvious mistakes I saw all around me, and I wanted to write a book about it: this book. What you hold in your hands is the essential guide for leveraging the processes and insights that I've gathered to help companies large and small, in industries and sectors far and wide, identify and act on their blind spots. Here are the vital tools to uncover your million dollar blind spots, which stem from financial or operational mistakes, management behavior, or poorly applied technology. Any functional department has the potential to create or correct million-dollar obstacles. Blind spots are opportunities and risks, and you can anticipate, eliminate, or control them.

This is where you come in. As an executive, are you asking the right questions? Are your people sharing with each other—and you—the right information? Have you earned your seat at the leadership table? I wrote this book for the leadership team: board members, the chief executive officer, and the C-level heads of each business function (sales, marketing, finance, operations, technology and human resources). This book treats your business with a physician's discipline and shows you where making simple but profound changes—educating yourself on best practices and evaluating your business across the board—will lead to a happier, healthier and longer business life

By following this guide you'll begin to put more money in your pocket. Build on the information in this book to lock down real numbers, useful metrics, honest assessments, supercharged management teams, unflinching accountability, and a healthy corporate culture. And you'll live the life you want.

Millions of dollars are hiding in the company's books. I examine how organizations interpret their balance sheet, and I'll help you do the same. I helped one company solve a $30 million inventory problem and avert a spectacular catastrophe.

Millions of dollars are falling into recurring cash sinkholes. I've shown conglomerates' executive teams how to change their accountability and bonus structures, and assign responsibility to deliver results from investment decisions.

Millions of dollars are spent on the wrong technologies. I demonstrated to a billion-dollar technology company that its advanced Oracle system wouldn't deliver timely, usable data as long as the company maintained forty separate legacy database subsystems.

How this book works

- **Chapter 1** starts you off on the right foot and gives you the top ten enterprise risk management questions that you'll need to understand problems, symptoms and opportunities at your business.

- **Chapters 2 through 9** unpack pitfalls and potentials in marketing, sales, human capital, and the CEO/CFO partnership. These two-chapter sections are designed to give you the lay of the land and the skills you'll need to craft your winning action plan.

- **Chapter 10** is your Million Dollar Blind Spots fiscal fitness health test, consisting of 20 questions designed to save your business;

- **Chapter 11** ties it all together with tools to help you realize your personal and professional goals, take hold of your future, and work from smart, real-world figures.

- **Chapter 12** is a bonus stress test you'll need to undertake the next steps in your organization.

Each section starts with a chapter on **core truths** that showcase what a C-level executive might erroneously assume everyone else on the organizational chart already knows. Then it puts theory into practice. Each section also includes **12 tips for working with each functional area**. Think of these tips as guidance on doing more with less within that function, and on communicating constructively about the stuff that matters. Along the way, in this book's expert Q&As, **eight experts in their field**, CEOs, executive directors, and business owners of organizations across the country, share their hard-won insights into managing and operating successfully given that resources are always limited.

Finally, this book is stocked with a solid personal coaching **resource section** to help you shepherd new million-dollar opportunities into reality. Put these real-world tools to work on the three issues you feel are most important to achieve success and you'll move further away from the starting gate, and further ahead than the competition.

Think of the value you'll derive from selling more, further, faster, with more customer value, and with more engaged, motivated, and aligned employees. Think of the value you'll derive from accelerating revenue growth for a new product in the next year. This book shows how you and your leadership team can work together, possibly for the first time, to nail the numbers and fund your own way forward.

You define your millions. They can mean a substantial percentage of sales. In fact, if the company's sales are *only* one million dollars, you're really talking about thousands, at least in the short term. Pay attention to your numbers, use them to help you grow, and one day your sales will hit millions--or even billions.

When we discuss "the CEO" or "boss," imagine your boss's boss. If you adopt the frame of reference of your boss's boss, you will increase your alertness to the big picture, and help you deliver more salient information where it's needed. It doesn't matter whether your company is public or private, large or small. Apply these truths across the board, and save money.

My expectation is that you'll refer to this guide often in the future, particularly when you are evaluating business challenges from a variety of new and valuable perspectives. You'll unlock ways to turn your functional area into a dynamic engine for growth, drive revenue gains, and spark more profitable communication with your boss and your boss's boss.

Use this book to learn how to earn your seat at the table.

Communicate strategically

Each chapter reminds you how to communicate effectively, strategically, with those around you. (We've chosen the male gender pronoun, but we mean both men and women). The best way to accomplish that is to begin each day at work by putting yourself in your boss's position—and in his boss's position, to the best of your ability. Odds are your boss is thinking:

- I need to know...
- I don't know...
- Why aren't you telling me?
- How can I help you tell me?

Help them fill in the blanks. Help your business sell more, provide higher customer value, attract and retain top talent, account for profits and losses, and lead its industry. Be generous with information. Be curious about solving problems. Be brave in your approach to teamwork.

- Do you have the courage to share information?
- Do you have the creative curiosity to seek it out?
- Do you have the passion to power through fear, and shatter limitations?
- Are you willing to share the glory when you succeed?

Whatever your functional area, consider the following:

- You know your functional area of expertise. Do you know the core truths of other functional areas? Do you understand their mission the way you understand your own?
- Do you have the courage, conviction, and confidence to share your department's core strengths and to help other departments work with you, not against you?

- Do you believe you and your department have value to offer other departments?

You have more power than you realize. There is free money all around you—potentially millions of dollars beyond insurance. I'm looking forward to helping you find it.

Let's get started.

Chapter 1

Free Up That Million Dollars Beyond Insurance

You can't know everything, but you can anticipate your company's risks and plan to neutralize or manage them. You'll be rewarded with reduced uncertainty and sustainable business performance that your stakeholders can count on.

We face personal risk every day, from small decisions we make (whether to hit the snooze button on the alarm clock and potentially oversleep), to large forces beyond our control (whether to get in the car knowing that a number of people are tragically killed in motor accidents every day). Because they are substantially more complicated, businesses face myriad risks on a major scale, but the options you have to deal with them, both as a person and as a corporation, are identical. It all comes down to your making informed choices based on your comfort with risk. Think of it this way: An insurance company may pay on losses from a car accident, but you won't look to an insurance company to bail you out if you oversleep and miss an important meeting. You have to prevent or manage that sort of risk on your own.

In the bigger picture, because the people in your organization may not be communicating with each other and you about the right things, you face massive exposure to non-insured risk. This is what I mean by strategic blind spots. Managing that risk can easily net you $1 million beyond insurance. What don't you know? Why aren't your people sounding that alarm? This book prepares you and your organization to take charge of risks, many of which are opportunities in disguise. But you have to watch for them, talk about them, and be ready to take informed, decisive action.

At the back of this book, I give you a suite of resources you can use to test your approach to risk and growth, and to set dramatically successful action plans. Between here and there: a wealth of knowledge and best practices for you and your entire leadership team. Put these to work and save the day.

Understanding risk

In the enterprise, we discuss risks in these categories: compliance-related, financial, operational, reputational, and strategic. And there is a strategic system for identifying risks, deciding how many and what kinds we can live with, and deciding how many and what kind we wish to prepare for or eliminate. This system is called Enterprise Risk Management, or ERM.

Think of this discussion as a way to develop a "beer budget" approach to managing risk in your operations and avoiding multi-million dollar mistakes by using common sense versions of risk management tools and risk assessment tools. The need is great because haphazard or nonexistent risk management is all too common. Look at the lessons in the rubble: the cost to recover after failed strategies at Netflix and on Wall Street; Japan's earthquake, tsunami, and nuclear woes; BP's Deepwater Horizon debacle in the Gulf of Mexico and beyond. Each calamity presents textbook lessons on risk, and each affects lives, livelihoods, and reputations.

Did those in charge do what they could in the face of risk? How will history rate your performance, should your organization take a hit? Get ahead of uncertainty now. You may not get a second chance.

The world we live in

It's been an interesting period as globalization has increased foreign exchange risk and has led to high-profile control failures. Many of us remember two vivid examples: the shocking destruction of London-based Barings Bank in 1995 by a lone employee who lost $1.3 billion of the firm's money in speculative investing; and the 2001 implosion of the

---

Think Fast. You Might Not Get a Second Chance

Talk about having the rug pulled out from under you.

Eileen was the new CEO of a high-tech company, the darling of the Street. They'd just raised $100 million—the day before the dotcom crash. What to do? Eileen's new company's business model, which had made it extremely successful, had to change, radically, and fast: ninety days fast, or overnight, in business terms.

Step one: sweep the champagne off the table. Step two: haul out the financials and get a fast read of the strategy challenge: how to immediately and properly understand our product costs and capacity to adjust the business model. We had to change pricing levels to set and increase customer profitability. Giving the product away wasn't an option.

Our solution was elegant. We redefined the business offering into three separate options, each of which made for a more nimble and varied approach to service and price points, creating exciting customer value, while preserving opportunities for growth.

This required obtaining operational- and Internet-activity non-financial information, which had never been part of the conventional accounting system. It also required data from siloed business functions, all of which thought their department had the answer on core customer costing and capacity data (they were incorrect).

Outside, the stock price was plummeting after the recent IPO. Inside, we pored over real-world, accurate, and actionable data, and trusted that our plan would stabilize the business and save the company. It did.

Shortly thereafter, eBay acquired the company, winning a business technology it needed and at a fair price. We kept the remainder of the $100 million.

We had the right numbers at the right time. We put them to work.

What are you missing or overlooking?

Houston-based energy, commodities, and services company, Enron Corporation, over a preventable scandal that also took down the Arthur Andersen accounting firm.

Moreover, new technologies complicate as well as simplify, whether on strategy issues or cyber terrorism. The enterprise faces risks and uncertainties that have less to do with its core mission and more to do with its own protection in order for it to compete. Consider the impact of Netflix's 2011 strategic decision to divide the company into separate physical and streaming divisions, mess with a winning brand, and raise prices in a brutal economy. They lost 600,000 to one million customers. To its credit, the company admitted that it dropped the ball in handling public relations and subscriber complaints.

The fact is, rating agencies, stock exchanges, institutional investors, and corporate governance demand senior executives to shoulder more responsibility for managing risks for the enterprise as a whole. And public shareholders reasonably expect stable, predictable, and positive financial performance. No, you can't know everything. But you have no excuse not to own your risk management.

In the following 10 brief discussions, we consider ERM, choice, and getting what you want.

1. What is Enterprise Risk Management (ERM) and why does it matter?

Entities exist to realize value for their shareholders, and management works to enhance, maintain, and encourage it in its strategy and execution of day-to-day operations. ERM helps management deal with uncertainty, giving them the tools they need to increase the upside.

To that end, ERM is a strategic program leveraging the attention and talent of everyone in an organization. Many businesses invest in an ERM program office charged with focusing on governance, control, assurance, and risk management. But even smaller or growth-scale organizations can make similar investment, if not in staff, then certainly in vision.

ERM requires a broad and deep scope of effort that relates to an organization's business objectives. Its role is to see that resources and controls are in place such that a reasonable person could expect that it would meet the firm's objectives. It is designed to identify risk—potential events that may upset the enterprise—and manage it according to the company's risk appetite, deriving from management's philosophy toward risk. That appetite is reflected in a company's overall strategy. For example, a startup often has a greater appetite for risk as it seeks high returns where success is uncertain; a mature firm might seek smaller but more stable return for its investors.

2. What are the initial elements of an ERM program?

As with other strategies, ERM leadership must come from the top, where the firm will set its risk philosophy, culture, and approach. ERM establishes an overall risk management philosophy with the understanding that both expected and unexpected events will demand an organization's resources, and that it's always better to react swiftly, surely, and correctly than to flounder about in confusion and let others frame your problem. ERM covers everything from workers compensation claims to natural disasters.

Armed with ERM, management keeps its finger on the pulse of its organization's risk culture, and evaluates how the organization's plans and actions affect its risk profile. For example, a business unit may weigh an unusually risky venture. Through ERM, top management knows of the opportunity and its costs—both planned and potential—and has evidence that the gamble will not undermine the firm's overall business objectives.

ERM also helps management account for risk strategy when setting organizational objectives. It reflects the explicit risk appetite of the entity and informs in the aggregate just how much risk the firm's management and board are willing to tolerate.

3. What other elements of an ERM program are necessary?

Identify your risk events (potential risk from unforeseen events associated with your company).

Plenty can go wrong inside and outside the enterprise to derail an organization's strategy and prevent it from meeting its business objectives. ERM weighs how these incidents could combine and interact to affect the company's overall risk portfolio. ERM harnesses powerful quantitative and qualitative methodologies to assess the probability and impact of each event, giving the smart firm options to follow before, during, and after times get tough.

It's a dynamic process and remarkable to see in action. Thoughtful and accurate ERM weighs the company's risk appetite, its cost benefit of response alternatives, and the extent to which a response diminishes the impact or likelihood of a particular risk.

Key to any ERM program is a system using internal controls, compliance with the separation of financial duties, quality control, and regulatory requirements. The company must capture and disseminate information in a form that allows individuals to carry out their jobs. For example, companies that mandate discrimination and sexual harassment avoidance training normally suffer fewer claims in these areas. If companies maintain smart protocols in hirings, firings, and complaints, they'll enjoy big savings in avoiding suits and claims. Be methodical. Eliminate problems before they are problems.

The last critical piece of the puzzle is a robust, ongoing monitoring of program elements, with follow-up by management and periodic review as tolerances and other variables will change. If your internal controls work and you've educated your department heads in the critical need to share information (more on that in the following chapters) you'll have the necessary elements of an effective ERM program.

4. What is an organization's appropriate risk context?

Think of risk context as an entity's risk threshold. More risk than this and a particular action becomes "risky." Less risk than this and we deem the issue consistent with the firm's objectives. For example, within an organization, the risk context for a new venture can differ for each manager depending on where he sits. That is, the risk context for an organization's geographical manager may be one of slow but stable earnings growth; the risk context for a product line manager in the same organization may be one of high but fluctuating returns. Which should be the risk context for the new venture?

Neither the geographical manager nor the product line manager's risk appetite is compelling, in and of itself. The risk context for the new venture is of the enterprise as a whole, from the view of the shareholder, employee, or customer.

5. How does an organization develop a risk culture?

One size doesn't fit all in ERM. The organization's management team must get together on what constitutes risk and require buy-in from everybody in the organization. Your people's talent, commitment, and cooperation will bring your

ERM guiding principles to life. And you have to give your team the tools to succeed. You'll educate them, support them, communicate with them, and reward them for their risk-smart behavior. If employees embrace the risk culture, they can help develop risk practices within their spheres of expertise. From their unique vantage point, they'll be your eyes and ears in detecting and reporting hidden risks in routine operations.

Naturally, this initiative must come from the top. The board of directors is responsible for senior management establishing risk management strategies. It is critical to the development of a risk culture that ERM be articulated at the senior management level. Your board and senior management will cooperate to ensure ERM's implementation throughout the organization.

When a company is large enough to justify full-time internal expertise to develop, monitor, and manage risk, it will benefit from the establishment of a chief risk officer. The CRO, ideally serving at the executive level, fosters dialogue throughout the organization and takes point on compliance. Line management performs the initial risk analysis, and the organization implements ERM infrastructure. This trusted person will incorporate risk controls into business decisions to protect the company from inappropriate risk exposure.

Risk management culture does require investing in human and financial resources, but in terms of risk avoided, messages owned, and employees made to feel integral to the operation's success, you're bound to come out ahead every time.

6. How do we categorize potential risk events?

The risk assessment must reflect the entity's objectives and its risk appetite. A portfolio view, which considers risks in the aggregate for the organization as a whole, provides the context for placing particular risk events in a logical category.

Risk category has two dimensions: potential impact and likelihood of occurrence.

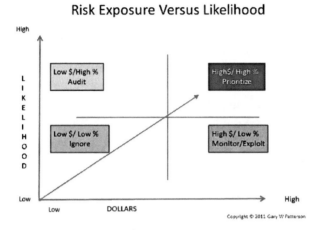

Risk Exposure Versus Likelihood

Using this graph (see fig. 1.1), let's populate the four quadrants using the following examples in a hypothetical corporation for risk events and a given set of risk dimensions:

- **High impact–high probability:** credit risk or product obsolescence
- **Low impact–high probability:** data entry errors or equipment obsolescence
- **High impact–low probability:** loss of communications capability or an earthquake
- **Low impact–low probability:** lost records or power outage at a noncritical facility

Categorizing a particular risk depends on the nature of the firm's business. For example, credit risk for a seller of earthmoving equipment may be high impact–high probability, while credit risk for a direct seller of children's clothes may be low probability–low impact. The impact, probability, and the nature of a company's business all determine how we categorize a particular event.

7. What are the different types of risk responses?

Like people, business entities enjoy a range of options in responding to a particular risk. Decisions about risk response within an organization that has effective risk management are made in the context of a firm's risk appetite and a portfolio view of risks in the aggregate. Here are the four types of risk response from which a company may choose:

- **Avoidance:** Stop engaging in the activity that creates the risk.
- **Reduction:** Reduce the probability and/or the impact of a particular risk.
- **Sharing:** Spread the risk among other entities.
- **Acceptance:** Do nothing and subject the firm to the risk event.

Avoidance might include declining to bribe foreign officials, thereby precluding the risk of regulatory prosecution. Reducing risk includes improving quality control to avoid a product recall. Insurance and hedging are classical examples of sharing the risk. And if you fail to implement security practices against the threat of terrorism, you've simply accepted that risk.

Within ERM, each company has a menu of choices, appropriate for them, from which to plan responses to events in their risk portfolio. It's worth pointing out that doing nothing—accepting risk—is still a deliberate choice.

8. What about ERM and IT?

Information technology provides data, reports, and management information; and it belongs in any effective risk management program, not just ERM serving high-tech firms. Think about it: how secure do you want the IT controls that are charged with processing your paycheck to be? Payroll security concerns have been around for so long that risk management normally works extremely well in this part of the IT world. Of course, IT reaches deeper into the enterprise than simply running payroll. Your company needs to protect and secure software code and confidential customer and process data assets, all well within the scope of a strong ERM program.

Moreover, when companies write their own code, they face trade secret issues. They must prevent staff or contractors from using or adapting proprietary code without permission. Developers must agree in writing to respect the firm's ownership. Some companies mark their software in ways that are invisible to you, but are clear as a fingerprint to them in order to protect from theft of their intellectual property and aid in its legal prosecution. If your company publishes proprietary code, consider such protection. If your company buys off-the-shelf or custom programming, review your contract indemnification.

Open-source code invites modification and comes from a culture of sharing; it presents its own set of problems. If the company modifies open code and now claims it as proprietary, inform your legal department. Challenges could emerge regarding your right to use a core piece of software. Companies also are obligated to limit access to vendor-licensed code by sharing it only with employees who are required to use it.

In addition to managing the risk associated with computer code, you must protect and secure confidential data.

QUESTIONS & ANSWERS

Harvey Koeppel |
Executive Director, Center for CIO Leadership
New York City

Harvey Koeppel is executive director of the Center for CIO Leadership, an international, cross-industry peer community focused on the advancement of business competencies for technology professionals through peer insights and connections, education, and research. He also is president at Pictographics, Inc., a sole proprietorship. From May 2004 through June 2007, Harvey helped lead Citigroup, both as chief information officer and senior vice president of its Global Consumer Group.

Gary Patterson: Harvey, how did you manage finite resources and take best advantage of business opportunities in your tenure at Citigroup and elsewhere, and what lesson can we take from that and apply to our organizations?

Harvey Koeppel: Basically, at a high level, the strategy involved self-funding. Going back to the CFO or CEO and saying I need another $5 million to do X, Y, or Z was often not a good idea. It's what we call a C.L.M., or a career-limiting move.

Anything new and significantly different we wanted to do, unless it was something that was so strategic and so innovative that it was going to change the landscape of the business (with all due respect, I don't think compliance and risk management fits that category) the goal really was about self-funding. If I wanted to spend $5 million on some piece of technology to increase the strength of our encryption, or create better firewalls, or whatever it might have been, I would look for opportunities to save money in once place, and typically took the savings and reinvested in the risk management function, or whatever it happened to be. This let us continue to do new stuff.

GP: How did that work? What did it look like?

HK: The technique generally was to look for savings through operational efficiencies or eliminating redundancies or whatever the case may be. If the amount was significant enough I'd generally cut a deal with the CFO and say, "Look, I'm about to save $10 million, I'll give you $7 million, but I need to keep $3 million for my work in wherever." He was happy to get $7 million back, and I was happy to not only improve the process, but also have $3 million more to spend on doing something else better.

GP: OK, but Citigroup is just huge. Is that approach going to work for most businesses?

HK: Part of it was size and scale for sure, but I would not say that this strategy would not work in a smaller organization. Of course at some level, it you have five people in an organization, and you're trying to cut a headcount, you're talking 20 percent of your organization, and you can't really cut *half* a headcount; you've got to keep the other half. At some level of scale it just doesn't work; but I would say for any kind of higher-end, mid-size to large enterprise, that's a pretty common technique.

GP: Everybody wins.

HK: Self-funding, from an operational-save perspective, is a triple-win score, in that you've made something better, you've reduced the cost, and you've funded your investment in something else to make something else even better. So yes, it's a win-win-win, and everybody's happy.

GP: What trips up executives trying to self-fund?

HP: There obviously are other ways to do it. Lots of people will rearrange the deck chairs on the Titanic: *I've got five people. I need one person over here, but my ten people are already allocated, aka, the definition of scarce resources, so I just steal one person from my ten and move him over here, which of course leaves a gap in wherever I took that person from.* The results are generally commensurate with the small-mindedness of the approach.

Generally that just slows down or kills some other effort in favor of doing a different effort, which is perhaps a short-term gain but generally leads to medium-term pain and long-term disaster.

GP: What's the solution? How do you cut with the least trauma, and best effect?

HP: Even though there was redundancy that could be eliminated, it's not like there was no impact, whether it was eliminating people or eliminating applications where we may have had five different systems doing the same thing. I figured that out we could really get away with only having four. There's always the need to socialize and get a buy-in of the people who are using the system that's about to be eliminated, and ensure that they were on board and had help adapting.

So yes: it wasn't like I could simply cut and slash and burn and take that money and go spend it. Obviously,

I had to accommodate whatever it was I was making the change to. Generally, that wasn't a terribly hard thing to do, and frankly, as my budget came from the lines of business, they were happy to save the money too.

GP: How can people on leadership teams help each other and the company to succeed?

HK: The real underlying dynamic, Gary, is to approach this process from a collaborative partnership perspective among the CIO, the other function heads, and the line of business partners. So it's not technology versus the business, or the business versus technology, or the CIO versus the CFO or any of that stuff; it was much more, Here's what we need to get done as an organization, let's align behind what those goals and objectives are as they meet the strategy. Now let's just go get done what we need to get done. If there are places where we're crossing either functional or organizational boundaries, let's be good corporate citizens and include in the conversations and the plans all of the stakeholders, and the beneficiaries, and anybody who might be impacted by whatever the change is being made so they're all bought in up front.

That way you get their full support for whatever it is you need to do, as opposed to stopping a system, and then a month later getting some irate e-mail from a president of a division who wants to know why his system just got turned off. That's a very different style, and as you can imagine, very different outcome. And it sounds kind of obvious, but unfortunately, a lot of people, and a lot of companies, don't operate this way.

GP: Does this all boil down to, "Do more with less"?

HK: You said it best in the way you asked the original question: it's the economic opportunity of managing scarce resources and getting more done. I *hate, hate, hate* the phrase, "Do more with less." It's such a cliché for most people, and saying it feels sort of like chewing tinfoil. But it's a cliché for a reason. If done properly, there's the opportunity to create value without increasing the total cost, in the ways that I've described.

GP: So as a CIO, and in fact as executive director of the Center for CIO Leadership, what's your take on the role of the CIO in owning the process of optimizing corporate economic opportunity?

HK: There's still a pretty big chasm in the world of CIOs, and I think it's also reflected across the C-suite, where people will talk about three or four different categories of CIOs based on their operating styles and all that. And frankly I think a lot of that is people trying to make a science out of something that doesn't need to have a science around it.

At a minimum there is definitely the operational perspective, which is tactical: keeping the lights on and saving money; and there is definitely the enterprise leadership perspective, which assumes as table stakes the operational perspective. That's the starting point as opposed to the end point. And the real end point is enterprise leadership. All the examples I've been giving your are examples of how a CIO, who is in that side of the equation, functions as an enterprise leader as opposed to (merely) a manager of the IT cost center.

GP: What does the enterprise-leadership-aware CIO know that his buddy, the IT cost center manager, doesn't?

HK: There are millions spent on the wrong technologies, that's certainly a true statement, no doubt about it, but what that really implies is: "I've spent my $80 million; it didn't work. I pretty much wasted $80 million."

What that doesn't account for is the lost opportunity value of what we could have created had our $80 million project succeeded. And generally, that lost opportunity value would be defined in terms of another $200 million in revenue recurring year over year, or a 5 percent increase in customer satisfaction that gets quantified in however many millions you want to quantify it, or increasing retention, or what have you. All too often people stop short around the failed projects.

Whether they've just wasted $15 million—or $15, forget the millions—it doesn't matter. The point is they lose sight of the fact that the lost opportunity often has a bigger cost than the dollars spent.

Prior to taking on the CIO role, Harvey provided consulting services to CtiiFinancial, Citibank, and other Citi affiliates from 1986 to 2004. He was heavily involved in supporting the planning and integration of many of Citi's major acquisitions, including Travelers Insurance, Associates First Capital, European American Bank, and Golden State Bank. For more information, visit www.cioleadershipcenter.com.

Data on in-house systems needs to be encrypted and protected from hackers. Encryption makes the stolen data unreadable.

Understand the value of the data you're loading onto third party systems from an ERM perspective. Examine your company's agreement with the IT vendor regarding steps they're taking to guarantee promised privacy and confidentiality. Companies must be able to protect stakeholder confidentiality or face legal issues—and a devastating loss of confidence and reputation. Often the vendor insists on indemnification. Is this something that the company can live with? Make sure legal signs off.

Now consider information reports and sensitive information on your employees' computer screens. This is a job for security as well. And moving beyond your facility, the threat is stronger, as you're increasingly dealing with the virtual aspects of intellectual property—and risks in the cloud invisible to the human eye. ERM has its work cut out for it with IT, and making sense of and managing this risk is increasingly complex.

9. How can data analysis help detect collusion between buyers and vendors?

Collusion is a deep and widespread problem and a perfect subject for ERM. Today's business environment has increased the likelihood of employee fraud. Individuals are under financial pressures as never before. Companies are trying to do more with less, so you may see a failure in financial segregation of duties. And unseemly bonuses on Wall Street have prompted many line employees to figure, "Well, I may as well get mine."

Kickbacks are a major form of collusion taking place between procurement employees and company suppliers, wherein an employee receives cash or other forms of compensation in return for inappropriately influencing a company buying decision. This includes paying invoices for goods or services never received, rigging bids, or providing the supplier with inside bid information.

Collusion is hard to detect. However, data analysis can flag unusual trends such as the number of invoices from a vendor over time, and the amount of dollars spent for goods and services from a particular vendor over time compared to previous periods. This type of analysis highlights scenarios that require further investigation.

10. How does media relations figure in ERM?

Media relations is a critical part of crisis management, whether the issue is a fire, chemical spill or other accident. In a high-profile crisis, the firm bears a significant public relations risk, as British Petroleum figured out in the wake of the Deepwater Horizon accident in 2010, after its perceived cluelessness and arrogance led to the company's leadership being savaged in public opinion. With 11 lives lost, 17 employees injured, 4.9 million barrels of crude oil flooded into the Gulf of Mexico, regional tourism and fishing industries left shattered, and marine and wildlife habitats damaged, the debacle is a textbook case study on how not to respond to reporters. Hint: Don't say of the victims, "We care about the small people," as BP's chairman Carl-Henric Svanberg did on June 16, following his meeting with President Obama. In the aftermath, BP's shareholders and employees lost billions in brand value.

Shutting the media out when a crisis hits is a big—and common—mistake, as rumors and speculation will always fill a news vacuum, compounding a stricken company's problem. At best, the company will look like it's sticking its head in the sand; at worst, it will suggest guilt and create anger that it will also have to deal with or accept, at increased risk.

It pays to be as transparent as possible, but you're not necessarily better off by discussing liability or insurance. As part of a community, both the company and the media have a role to play, and it's in the company's interest to help the media do its job, even if the initial story is embarrassing. If you do this well, the story quickly will turn to how effective you are at rising to the challenge.

The smart company will safely escort news organizations to the crisis site and detail the measures it is taking to deal with the situation. Remember: transparency often enables the firm to win favorable light in the media and in public opinion. Get out in front of the story. Help answer questions such as who, what, where, when, how and why. Tell the story of your ERM success: You have a plan, the plan is working, and this won't happen again.

Consider that everyone in the company is in charge of managing your company's reputation. You may have heard parts but not all of the classic example of Johnson & Johnson's Tylenol crisis and its public relation program's successful handling of the cyanide poisoning. One less publicized part of the story deals with the question of how many executives have the courage of J&J's James Burke to turn to the company's code of conduct for guidance. J&J's founder, Robert Wood Johnson wrote in 1943, "Put simply, Our Credo challenges us to put the needs and well-being of the people we serve first." Decades later, J&J's handling of that crisis remains a standard bearer for how companies should handle a crisis. To refresh your memory, try a Web search of "public relations" and "Tylenol Crisis."

In this book, I periodically suggest that maintaining the courage, passion, perseverance of your convictions enables you to share the core and operational strengths of your department in order to help other departments. That's it. If you've evaluated your company's position relative to these Top 10

Enterprise Risk Management (ERM) questions, you're set to shepherd your company through certain and uncertain risks—and live to fight another day. Your best defense is to be methodical and execute your best practices.

***

The Bedrock Truths of Finding Your Million Dollars Beyond Insurance

- Set informed risk choices based on your comfort level.
- Encourage your people to share information.
- Understand your risk categories.
- Avoid, reduce, share, or accept risk. But know why you're choosing that.
- Secure your IT under ERM to limit exposure.
- Fight fraud with data analysis.
- Help the media do its job during crises.

Coming up:

So you think you "get" your marketing department? Without meaning to, these dedicated workers may be hiding millions from you. To jointly help uncover that money, let's look under marketing's hood and see what makes this department tick.

Chapter 2

Understanding Millions in Marketing: What Marketing May Not Be Telling You

Despite what many might think, marketing and sales are two different animals. If the heart of business is sales, then the heart of marketing is the strategy to drive those sales. Yes, there's an exception: at many companies, marketing and sales are run as one department. That means they focus on market definition and strategy, pricing and promotion, and marketing communication and campaigns. We'll get to this in Chapters 4 and 5 when we discuss promise and progress in the digital advertising space.

There's a magic to marketing: an amalgam of art and science that turns the understanding of customer need and desire into cold cash: your profits. When the marketing department slips in selling its core strengths and bedrock expertise within the enterprise, it costs the team big money. Other departments must understand what marketing does, and how to leverage that information to work together more profitably.

In this chapter I'll walk you through marketing's turf, and get you up to speed on several key concepts and practices that will drive extra millions of revenue growth to accelerate scaling your business. Experienced marketers, use this chapter to help you consider how you can help break down functional silos and keep the boss informed, enlightened, and singing your praises.

Success in marketing begins in excelling at creating and designing the product or service you bring to market (*Will the dogs eat the dog food?*) Of course, today we have to do it faster, at less cost, and with better results that can be measured and monitored. Competition is intense. So marketing should analyze the market and competition, and devise the statements that explain why our widget is better for the customer than the other guy's; or why the customer will be cooler, hipper, and happier with our widget. Why is it to the customer's advantage to go with us? Why are we the brand he wants to identify with? That's marketing.

How effective are your marketing people at optimizing salespeople's time in front of prospects?

Ansoff Product/Market Matrix

Experienced sellers are familiar with the relatively new Ansoff product/market growth matrix, which orients organizations to think about revenues depending on its offerings. It yields solutions for marketing new and existing products in a new or existing market space. It's powerful and straightforward. The Ansoff approach lets businesses plan progress on paper before committing to the real thing—and spending substantial amounts of money. This approach helps find the strategy that presents the least amount of risk to your organization. So whether you are a young corporation or a titan in your field, consider the benefits of Ansoff to tailor your marketing approach to target customers.

Let's get more visual with the following diagram (table 2.1) of the Diversification aspect of the Product/Market Ansoff matrix.

		Products	
		Present	New
Markets	Present	Market penetration	Product development
	New	Market development	Diversification

After you consider where you stand in these relationships, weigh these questions (table 2.2)…

Existing Product/Service to Present Market:	New Product/Service to Present Market:
- Does this offering require increased consumption from customers, or are you taking market share from competitors? How? - How do you attract existing customers? Why would they come? - What might competitors do to try to stop you?	- Is this something that customers want? - Do they need it? - What does your offering replace? Why is your solution a better choice? - How do you communicate your value to customers? Why should customers believe you?
New Product/Service to New Market:	**Existing Product/ Service to New Market:**
- Is your offering really new or are others offering something similar you just don't know about? - Has it been tried before and abandoned as unworkable? - Who are your customers? How do you find them? - What do you say to them when you find them? - How do you define your customers' needs? - How does you product/service satisfy those needs? - How do you prove those customers exist? - How do you prove your product/service will satisfy customers' needs?	- How do you prove that you're needed where you want to do business? - How do you prove demand is waiting for you when you get there? - Now that you've established the market, which competitors are set to follow with the same product at a lower price and better service? What will you do about it?

Even after you develop your strategy, you're in for some heavy lifting. (And the rewards that brings.)

The Art of Bootstrapping

We're not picking on marketing or sales if we say that in today's business environment, and for the foreseeable future, the mandate is, "Do more with less." One of my clients keeps a great sign outside his office door that basically warns visitors what they had better ask themselves before they ask him for money:

- Do you really need to buy it?
- How long can you wait before buying it?
- How can we get it cheaper when you have to buy it?

Notice he's not saying you *can't* have it, or must reduce quality, or don't ask. He's simply driving home the need to make the best use of the company's money. How can your business inspire employees to care as much about cash efficiency?

An entrepreneurial mindset can exist in companies of any size. In fact, it is so prevalent in larger companies that the phenomenon of acting like an entrepreneur inside a larger organization is called "intrapreneurship."

Bootstrapping means doing more with less. Regardless of your company's size, it must excel at this. Young and scrappy entrepreneurs bootstrap as a matter of necessity; middle-market and larger companies must not forget these early survival lessons.

Marketers have always had to dig, scratch, and claw out their budget, so let's acknowledge them as entrepreneurs. To the extent that your employer sees marketing as primarily an expense center, learn to develop some numbers to back up the results of your work that help demonstrate marketing return on investment. After all, the seat at the leadership table goes to marketers who think strategically *and* can talk about the numbers accurately and confidently.

By now you should be paying attention to ideas and steps that will help you survive the critical, capital-deprived days of your enterprise, and make note of techniques for proving your business case and growing yourself sales.

Consider that your boss's boss is an investor in the strategy and tactics *you* propose. He or she is investing in financing that other people also want a piece of as well as valuable time—their own, their peers' and their subordinates'—in implementing your proposals. Along with mastering this capital expenditures (CAPEX) logic, follow up on how well the project actually turns out so you can learn more and refine your approach and execution for better results. People want to trust you with resources. Help them to do so.

We can apply bootstrapping to our business models. These are some characteristics:

- Low up-front capital requirements
- Short sales cycle (less than a month)
- Generally payment terms (less than a month)
- Recurring revenue
- Word-of-mouth advertising

Managing for cash flow means passing up sales that are profitable but might also take a long time to collect, and it means always viewing the money used to prime sales as if it were your own.

Once you've got money coming in, then you can safely invest more on longer-term initiatives, and invest months of stately planning and analysis in other projects

Are you bootstrapping? You should be.

Market research: Build a Bottom-up Forecast

No bootstrapper in his right mind would build a top-down forecast by calculating how much of a market one needs to succeed. Typically, entrepreneurs start with a large number (e.g. "the global market for widgets is $100 billion") and extrapolate projected sales down from that figure. For example, let's say you want to crack the Internet access market for China. Here's a pie-in-the-sky top-down plan, which would make the CEO, board of directors, or banker cringe:

- China's population is estimated at 1.4 billion.
- 20 percent of this population want Internet access.
- We will secure 10 percent of that potential audience.
- Each account will yield $240 per year.
- Size of the market is $1.4 billion × 10 percent address-able market x 20 percent success rate × $240/customer = $67 million per annum.

Not a bad haul. Of course, it's total rubbish. No business would aim for such a return without proof customers will buy from them at all. Most experienced leaders see through it as hype. Admit it, though, you have seen versions of this approach in the wild. I know I have.

Bootstrappers don't build top-down models, but rather bottom up-models, beginning with real-world variables:

- For simplicity, assume the number of complete phone pitches a telemarketer can make in one day (30).
- The number of prospects who qualify as potential customers is 30 percent.
- There are 240 business days in a year.
- A telemarketer can close sales on 10 percent of qualified prospects.

- 30 calls/day × 30 percent sales prospects × 240 days/ year × $240/customer (noted earlier) = $500,000/ annum/telemarketer.

A team of 10 salespeople, according to our bottom-up model, can thus produce $5 million in revenues. You can argue the conversions and assumptions, but it's possible to settle on proof. This model offers real-world projections for cash flow and costs (number of prospects, number of salespeople, and so forth).

Are you looking at your problem top-down or bottom-up? Which do you think is more realistic?

Use Prototypes as Market Research

If you have a good business idea, prototype a small model of it and see if it works. Remember the success of Pierre Omidyar, founder in 1995 of eBay, which in 2011 boasted annualized operating sales of $11 billion. This business became a multi-billion-dollar business because Omidyar believed his company could make money by creating a community of local buyers and sellers, an idea he scaled up from flea markets, garage sales, and newspaper classifieds. Omidyar's community grew and in short order, users all over the world were hooked.

Prototyping made it possible. Omidyar prototyped his idea for a direct person-to-person auction on his own computer, and launched his enterprise from his apartment using free Web space. He collected a small fee for every transaction. The design was clean, straightforward, and bulletproof. Then he moved to a working demo and turned it loose on the market to prove it worked, got financing, and ramped up dramatically.

The business model was simple:

- Find a strategy that brings buyers and sellers together with a common objective.

- Create a method generating a revenue stream from transactions between the buyers and sellers.
- Create operational features that help buyers and sellers readily commit in a secure environment.

Your new product or service might also capture lightning in a bottle, but odds are you're not going to know what the buying public has an appetite for until you commit some resources. During these times, conventional market research falls flat. You have to run some small market test.

Your wisest choice: Take your best shot with a prototype. Go to market immediately. Sell something and learn quickly with customer feedback, positive and negative. Revise as needed until you have what real customers will buy at a profit. Otherwise, the market will cheerfully pass you by while you plan, wait, cogitate, seek advisors, and hold out for ideal circumstances to launch.

This ready, fire, aim and recalibrate is where marketing excels.

The expected outcome of this "get going" principle is a first release of a product or service. It will not be perfect, but revision based on customer feedback means that the next round of customers will have a better experience than the first. Speak to successful business people. You'll often learn that that their biggest regret likely was in waiting as long as they did to get products or service into customers' hands.

The benefits of getting your product or service to market rapidly: immediate cash flow and real-world feedback. More than that, you have something to *talk* about. Now marketing people can write about real world experience. Some customer who adores you will welcome you to write a case study. Some media channel looking for something interesting will give you visibility if you pitch it to its target audience.

Some Research Required

What if your product stumbles? How can you limit risk in this test market?

- Does your product or service, at this stage of development, leapfrog or differentiate from the competition?
- Can you test market into a remote area or segment to limit fallout?
- Do you have a tolerant and understanding customer group of willing guinea pigs (as is arguably the case with Apple's loyal early adopters)?
- Does your product or service meet most of the needs for most users?
- Have you done enough "in vitro" testing (for example friends, family, colleagues, alpha and then beta) to help you figure out what the real world thinks?

How to Analyze Your Industry

Regardless of an entrepreneur's size or reach, when developing business plans, each must establish the size of their markets. Avoiding unrealistic projections is a major challenge. Entrepreneurs must state in their plans a realistic projection of their addressable market. Convincing, documented, real-world numbers carry more weight than do general/broad industry figures.

The challenge for you is to temper your enthusiasm, particularly if you see niche and developing markets as a huge opportunity. You want to establish yourself as a market leader. You may be at philosophical odds with your board of directors, which has seen too many risky adventures in new markets. Boards are usually more comfortable with a proven medium-sized market than an untapped niche.

To answer those concerns, conduct a market analysis, often referred to as market potential. Say you're a sales person who believes in the potential of the general market for pizza mini-ovens. Food is a highly visible and dynamic market, offering the highest employment potential of any industry. You need to peel back the onion of potential to get at the core address-able part of the market, which is genuinely accessible to the business.

Who else is competing for your customer? What products and services do they offer? What are alternatives for your prospects? Your research should uncover who else may enter your niche marketplace, and how long it would take them to arrange production, supplies, and distribution. Depending on your nice product, consider patent protection.

For Business Planning, Competition is Good

How do you define competition? Does it align with your internal investor's (your boss's boss) views? Investors define competition as any service or product that a customer can use to fulfill the same need(s) as the company fulfills, including businesses that offer like products, alternate products, and other customer options—for example, carrying out the service or constructing the product themselves. What are the alternatives for your prospects? Don't forget the customers' option to do nothing.

Direct and Indirect Competition

A business plan has to take into account a business's direct and indirect competitors.

Direct competitors are the business's competitors, who are trying to attract the same target market. **Indirect competitors,**

QUESTIONS & ANSWERS

Keith Kantor |
CEO, Service Foods, Inc.
Norcross, Ga.

Keith Kantor, PhD, is owner and CEO of Service Foods, Inc., a middle-market health and wellness community whose three brands, Service Foods, Blue Ribbon Foods, and Southern Foods at Home, employ some 200 people. Together they provide gourmet, all-natural food that is both healthier and better tasting than the food many of us can find at a local grocery store, and deliver everything to customers' homes free of charge.

Moreover, Service Foods routinely wins plaudits and awards from the likes of the Natural Product Association, Ernst & Young, Business Leader Magazine, Georgia Trend Magazine, *and the* Atlanta Business Chronicle, *who tout the company's excellence in entrepreneurship, industry leadership, and smart growth.*

Gary Patterson: Keith, you're a retired Marine Corps officer used to getting things done directly, efficiently, and effectively. Your success in running your company has freed you to start working toward reforms in the U.S. healthcare industry that your blue ribbon advisory report says would save lives—and $333 billion within 10 years.

Keith Kantor: It's staggering. Those savings amount to nearly 15 percent of our total health-care costs of $1.8 trillion. As you can see if you go to the report [available by PDF at Service Foods's website], these savings come from simple, non-controversial methods. That doesn't even count the large savings to be gained from reduced absenteeism and higher productivity at work.

GP: Is health "baked" into your culture at Service Foods?

KK: Healthy living is the main focus at Service Foods, and it's not just for our clients' sake. We know how important it is for everyone to live a healthy lifestyle. We see our health and wellness programs as an investment in our employees and their families. We're all working together to improve the health of America, one family at a time. We were just named *Atlanta Business Chronicle*'s Healthiest Employer of the year for the second year running. We're a great place to work and have no turnover.

GP: You promote your company as "green," a claim to corporate environmental responsibility you can make confidently after subjecting yourself to an independent audit that helped you become 100 percent carbon neutral. Was all that work worth the expense?

KK: Absolutely. This was covered in the press: despite the recession, following these investments, we achieved a three-year revenue increase of 306 percent, and added 60 new jobs in the Atlanta area. We didn't do it just to be altruists; going green—I wish more businesses understood this—is a powerful marketing and sales lever. The response from customers was so enthusiastic that the additional volume actually offset any extra cost and made our product slightly less expensive. What I thought would be a 5 percent *increase* ended up being cost-neutral, or even pushed costs down 1.5 percent. In this industry, that's excellent.

GP: How do you lead this company? How do you solve problems?

KK: We've broken the company into several teams, akin to fire teams in the Marines, and these are small, fast, and flexible. Every week we have a team meeting, and the concept is to come up with solutions to any problem. But we say, "Don't tell me only the problem, tell me your solution." The people on the front line are the ones who are in the best position to come up with solutions, because they see what works. I review, as CEO, all their notes. We look at the choke points, what you're calling blind spots, and list these on a board. Which ones come up the most? What are, say, the top three? We reward our people for avoiding choke points through team bonuses, with contests, because that tends to free up time, which is money. A lot of money.

For more information on Service Foods' Blue Ribbon Advisory Panel:
Recommendations to Fix and Lower Costs in the U.S. Healthcare System *(2012), visit www.servicefoods.com/ my_health_info/blue_ribbon_advisory_panel_recommendations_to_lower_healthcare_costs.pdf.*

in contrast, are competitors who are trying to attract a different target market, with different products and/or services, or are trying to attract a different target market with similar products and/or services. Consider both, because your prospects may turn to either set of competitors, particularly if your competitor has an established mind share.

Note that successful entrepreneurs don't trivialize the competition: they speak solely to clearly present their point of difference in the market, and, eventually, to define their market. That's what's so nice about B2B marketing: you're solving problems, not trying to create a need you can fill with your product.

Investors aren't fools, at least not the ones we're talking about: competitors who have been in the market for some time have already proven their capacity to build market share; they will vigorously defend their market share, and have the business advantages of the high ground.

The most important areas of a market analysis are the business's competitive advantages over other suppliers, and competitors' identification of how these can be converted to actual wins as far as market share. Whereas a newcomer may face some barrier to entry, an incumbent needs to think about protecting their market share.

Sound financial assumptions and projections based on documented industry numbers—not naïve assumptions—communicate operational maturity and credibility.

Let's take a page from Mary Cole of B2B Technology Marketing, who seems to have a knack for pulling in accurate, solid numbers. You could spend thousands of dollars for a research study on your target market. Or you could visit a business library and research it yourself, with a business librarian's free assistance. Librarians are experts at finding things out, and they know which databases will yield the information you need and how to access them. You can gather this information at the library or at home, depending on database licensing agreements.

From directories and company information to market research to international resources and newspapers, periodicals and grants, business libraries are plump with information you can leverage for free, starting today.

For her part, Cole is a fixture at the Kirstein Business Library in Boston, which she describes as the best free research facility for entrepreneurs in eastern Massachusetts.

Market Power and Margins

Everyone would love for his business to enjoy fat operating gross margins. So would his banker. But financial projections and assumptions are a minefield for overly optimistic leaders.

If you are a manufacturer, or seek to establish a manufacturing business and show, say, 50 percent to 80 percent operating margins, you may find that investors will question your premises. It is relatively easy to access the operating margins of public manufacturers anywhere in the world, then simply go to the financial accounts and note the margins. They fall far short of 80 percent.

You can learn much about presenting your business by reading the published financial accounts of public companies in your market. The biggest challenge is that a public company generally extends into more markets with more products than private companies. This makes it difficult since you're comparing apples and oranges, but it's better than nothing. You need to measure yourself against something in the real world.

The Demands on Working Capital

A business plan to a savvy investor is like an X-ray to a surgeon. And as the surgeon learns precisely where to operate by reading the X-ray, so, too, does the CFO, CEO, and board of directors read a business plan to find an emerging business's promises and pitfalls.

They look for obvious clues. Is there really an opportunity here? Can these people pull it off? Will the cash flow meet projections?

Financial projections such as revenues, profit margin, and earnings can mislead, although not necessarily intentionally. Readers generally assume that projections are based on optimistic scenarios, so they expect to see the basis for assumptions. These bases should refer to actual sales in like situations where possible. If they are simply guesstimates, then that should be based on reliable assumptions. Business plans should provide in an appendix a description of the source of the data (and come equipped with illuminating footnotes). Again, documentation inspires credibility, and credibility inspires funding.

For example, 25 percent per annum growth in revenue might be a fair assumption for years one through three, but over ten years? Not so much. Investors and boards will call it unrealistic.

Highlight any shortfall on capital and plans to address them.

Validating Assumptions and Projections

Financial assumptions are the screws that hold the business case together. Make sure they're feasible. Let me repeat that:

The Power of a Question

Ask the wrong question and you might get the right answer, but for the wrong reason, and you'll be out of business in short order). Learn to ask the right question. That's golden.

Charlie was chairman of the European manufacturing arm of a publicly owned Fortune 500 manufacturer-distributor of industrial and building products. They'd been in business for more than a hundred years and were overdue for updating. Charlie, in his fifties, brought a strong engineering background and an MBA from a top school. He was tasked with moving his $150 million division from loss to profitability quickly and in a turbulent market.

It was a risky situation. It was just a matter of time before the market turned downward again, and his reporting system, looking

---

ever backward as it did, was ill-equipped to help him lead through tough times. Charlie's options appeared painfully limited.

Why? Manufacturing was almost blind on its supply chain. Sure, this company could, and did, create and file timely SEC reports, but if you'd asked them which customers or products were the most profitable, they had no idea. And it was going to cost them. Their accounting systems excelled at telling them where they had been, but failed at telling them where they were going until they got there.

How could Charlie essentially move his division beyond a Luddite society to a modern, savvy, and intelligent information system that let them look around corners? Or uphill? Or over the horizon?

We quickly created a way to accumulate useful product costing and job cost information, and our system immediately began feeding us essential, actionable reports on product winners and losers. We hauled butt back to profitability. It worked out well. The company is sailing into its second hundred years, riding a wave of intentional, not accidental, results.

Make sure your financial assumptions are feasible and include:

- Conversation rates
- Operating margins
- Headcount

Investors Want to See an Opportunity, not a Biography

What is your business opportunity? When an investor determines whether an idea has merit, he will generally want to fall back on industries and businesses he understands, and often will eschew poorly defined opportunities that require a leap of faith. Here are the essential features of a framework for determining and assessing an idea:

What is your market data?

- How big is the market? Local? Regional? Nationwide? Worldwide? What are you aiming for?
- How you define your market will depend on the problem you solve and the customer's other options.
- Know your competitors inside and out. What do they sell? For how much? How do they sell, directly or indirectly? Through which distribution channels?
- How can you reach your market? Where do these people go to solve their problem? Can you get in front of them at the time they need you?
- What worked 20 years or so ago probably won't work today. Today you need to be found online. What's your strategy for meeting your customers where they hang out?

How easily can someone find market data? A viable market question requires answering the size and potential of the market, and whether in addressing this market, the business can make an attractive return on investment.

Provide an honest description of all the known risks involved. When one opportunity is too complex to attack or understand, then it will probably also be too difficult to execute.

Not a Huge Market, Please

Here's how to turn off your boss, internal and external investors, lenders, partners and suppliers: Tell them you have no competitors and that you're going to be the market leader in an $800 billion industry.

Again, there's nothing wrong in relating your business to a successful existing business, but a perennial and annoying characteristic of many entrepreneurs is that they present large, generic market sizes as if that alone should get investors excited. It won't.

If you're offering a new type of product, the best you may be able to do is cite the market base you'll be selling into. You may not be able to predict what percentage of the market will bite. You know only so many are prospects, but how many of them will care? Hit the numbers from the bottom up. Triangulate the information from a variety of sources. Alternatively, if you suggest you're first in and best dressed with no competition based on your unique business case, well, is that a good thing? Is this really a comfortable position for you? Who really wants to be first? OK, it's politically incorrect, but vivid and generally true: You can tell who the pioneers are; they're the ones with the arrows in their backs.

If there are few companies in a particular market space, how can you determine that a market may just not exist, or determine that customers simply won't pay enough for the product or service for you to make money from the venture? Or even worse, customers have the option to do nothing? On the other hand, when there are already established companies in the space, it should be seen as a lower risk entry—one where others did not fear to tread. Then the issue becomes differentiation.

Investors want to see value, and they'll see through claims of large generic markets that are impossible to convert into customers.

Addressable Market
In our view, entrepreneurs should define their potential in terms of the addressable market: the actual percentage of the available segment.

For example, let's say you want to attack the pizza market. You've developed a super "mini" oven that offers advantages over larger, more expensive and inefficient ovens. Your oven is tailored to the more contemporary market for thinner (healthier) pizza, and can be fitted out in traditional restaurants, cafes, and shopping malls.

As already noted, the kind of modeling that starts with a large number and works down to extrapolate projected sales from that figure is generally of little use to an investor. If the market opportunity is attractive enough to satisfy your capital expenditures requirements process (CAPEX), it's better to build a bottom-up model.

Let's look at the pizza mini-oven case (hypothetically):

- There are 60,000 cafes and restaurants in your part of the United States.
- A salesperson can make appointments to see 25 potential customers in a week.
- These potential customers have already been qualified by a telesales phone call.
- There are 45 working weeks in a year.
- Five percent of the sales calls will convert to a purchase order within six months.
- Each sale is worth $8,000 to the business.
- The business founders could expect $225,000 in revenue in first six to nine months.

At that point, it's possible to see whether sales would increase sufficiently to justify your business moving forward on this product and if this would deliver an adequate profit margin for your overall costs and expenses.

Now you're in business.

To help build that business and exploit those missing millions in marketing, the next chapter will provide a dozen secret tips that are actually focused tactics to ensure you exploit the full benefits marketing can provide all areas of the business.

∗∗∗

Remember, the key to finding million-dollar blind spots is to ensure marketing provides maximum value. When the entire management team understands marketing's core truths (see below), marketing has earned or kept its seat at the table.

Bedrock Truths of Marketing

Spend money wisely.

Who is your customer?

Will they buy your product or service? Will the dogs eat the dog food?

Document, test, and validate assumptions.

Where does your customer go to solve their problem? How can you be sure you're there waiting for them?

Be flexible and embrace change. Marketing is a process.

View your boss's boss as investing money and people's time on your marketing plan recommendation.

Chapter 3

Uncover Millions in Marketing

Now that the full team has a grounding in the marketing department's bedrock concepts, let's focus on unleashing marketing's hidden millions. Our key goals are meeting customer expectations without giving away the store and retaining valuable customers.

Here's what I mean by valuable customers: It costs five to eight times more to gain a new customer than it does to retain one you already have. In a cash-strapped world, successful organizations know the value of holding onto existing customers rather than having to sniff out new ones. A word of warning: You won't get credit simply for knowing that you should do these things. You get credit for consistently implementing programs that follow these bedrock principles. Tweak these suggestions for your situation. Whatever you do, don't let your million-dollar blind spot be losing customers over satisfaction issues.

Marketers, highlight sections of this chapter to give your peers insight into propelling business profitability from your point of view. Non–marketers, guess what: you, too, are responsible for successful marketing. Apply these tips to help grow your bottom line.

Know the Score

Raising average revenue per customer depends on making products and services that people want to keep on buying. There are lots of ways to retain customers, but many of them are difficult and expensive; and we're not looking to spend money in this chapter, but save it. To that end, here are 12 low-cost "secret tips" for your use in improving your organization's return on effort, with examples:

Tip 1: Know what your customers want

It sounds obvious, but it's too often overlooked or gone about improperly. Find out what your customers really want. Don't just trust that they'll tell you the full story in a feedback form (they often ignore those or throw them in the trash). Special tip: if you can find out in a live interaction, even better. You need to be able to restate the customer's problems, state available solutions, and understand your cost of doing nothing.

—With clients, ask them often how things are going and what you can do to improve.

—If you're a brick and mortar operation, meet your customers at the front of the shop, or assign someone friendly and alert to do this for you. Walmart stores put their best foot forward at the door with their greeters. Get to know your customers. Who are they? Why did they come today? What are they looking for? Make that good impression. Make that valuable connection.

—If you're a Web-based business, you may well have to rely on feedback forms to glean customer details. Don't just read them, follow up with a telephone call or Twitter hit. Feedback forms aren't ideal, as I say, so you have to motivate your customers to use them, and maximize the value of the feedback you do receive.

One way to incentivize your customers to provide feedback is to offer them an incentive. For example, enter each respondent into a drawing for $100 or a free product in exchange for providing feedback. That's a small investment on your part, and you might learn a tremendous amount about how your business is doing and what your customers want.

To mix fun and function, host a mixer after hours to thank customers for their patronage. Serve appetizers and wine, and encourage them to network (this is an added value you are creating for them, incidentally). Not only will you have a chance to learn what people think of your business, your offerings, service, employees, and so forth, you will be able to form personal relationships between your employees and your customers. We all prefer to do business with people we know. You'll gain valuable intelligence you can put to work right away, and you'll forge lasting customer bonds.

No matter your approach to obtaining feedback, are you listening? Failure to listen is a mistake many leaders make, one that dooms organizations. Customers want to provide you with critical facts to improve or even save your business, but you have to listen for them. Small and (to you, perhaps) seemingly unimportant aspects of your offering could be the reason why customers stay away in droves, bad-mouth you online, or take a closer look at your competition.

If you're alert to what your customers want—if you adjust your products or services based on real-world feedback—you'll see huge gains in your ability to keep customers at minimum cost.

QUESTIONS & ANSWERS

Mary Cole |
B2B high tech global marketing consultant
Greater Boston area

Mary Cole is a business executive whose background includes Digital Equipment; Prime Computer; co-founding a successful software development company; angel investing; five years of financial services industry experience; and marketing and strategic development consulting to American and international corporations and universities.

As she explains, her interests lie in developing profitable markets for high-tech products and services by listening to prospective market participants, and laying the groundwork for what she calls "self-selecting prospects who turn into happy customers."

Gary Patterson: Where do your clients seem prone to blind spots, and what can they do about it?

Mary Cole: As a consultant, I encounter people coping with a subject they're least competent in. Otherwise they wouldn't have reached out to me. So I see a lot of blind spots. In my experience, when people try to address unfamiliar issues, they often come at it with a blindness characterized by their true expertise.

Here's an example: I worked with a couple guys I know who had been great executive salesmen in another life. They formed a company, looking to make a lot of money out of e-mail management software for organizations. They wanted me to help with "marketing." And my initial response was, "Let's talk to some people similar to the people you would sell to, and let's get their view of the problem that you solve. Let's understand their hot buttons, their pain points, and get a feeling for the product space in the real world."

So we did this a couple of times, and it became obvious that [my clients'] concept of marketing was [to find] somebody who could introduce them to potential customers. They didn't understand that marketing involves leverage, and sales involves the one-on-one gathering of revenue. Marketing always supports sales, but because their background was sales, they did not understand the leveraging component of marketing.

Immediately after hearing people describe their organization and what they were trying to do, my guys went into sales mode. They stopped listening. And they really never understood that that was totally inappropriate. We were there to gather information, and of course it caused me a bit of pain. These were people I knew, who trusted me, and I had not intended to set them up for this type of onslaught. I had requested meetings so we could learn from them, and what they got was, unfortunately, a hard sales pitch.

Sometimes as a consultant, you don't always have a perfect match with the client. You would like somebody to call and say, "I need this this and this done," with a sense that your client understands what marketing is and what it can do for them.

As you say, Gary, there are these million-dollar issues, these black holes that people are not aware of. If you're a marketing manager, it is your responsibility to make sure that other departments understand what marketing does. Marketing managers must also make sure that the company's marketing people understand what they bring to the party, what other departments bring to the party, and how the organization benefits when departments share information.

For example, marketing provides sales with the general market picture and specific leads; sales provides marketing with feedback on competitive evolution, on what worked, and what didn't work. It's all teamwork.

Mary Cole is on LinkedIn at http://www.linkedin.com/in/ marylcole, and blogs on marketing, politics, investments, and life at http://euonymous.wordpress.com.

Tip 2: Create anticipation for new products

When it comes to creating consumer need and anticipation for new products, you don't have to look beyond the shining example of Apple, Inc. Apple managed to sell more than 300,000 units of its new iPad in the first day of sales alone, and customers downloaded 250,000 eBooks that day from the iBookstore. Over the first weekend, Apple shipped a whopping 700,000 iPads. How? The company created a pitch of suspense so fevered people camped out in lines just for a chance to touch the latest iThing. Marketing hype, not necessarily just engineering, fed this desire, loyalty, and revenue.

You can do it too.

We've seen Apple's strategy applied time and again in the business world to retain customers, and to encourage them to buy the next in a series of products. Take the example of the movie industry. It convinces customers they must see the director's next installment as soon as it comes out. Regardless of the movie's quality, if the teaser trailer is phenomenal, people will be buzzing about it all over the Web. Seeing the film is inevitable, the gross receipts are tremendous, and that fuels the sequel.

Studios and publishers generate excitement for new products or services by spreading the word long in advance of the release date, and making preproduction itself an object of intense speculation in blogs, YouTube, Twitter, Facebook, chat rooms, and the press. Sneak peeks, Easter eggs, pre-orders, and exclusive content make the product release a force in the potential audience's lives. If you can create anticipation for your products and services, you'll keep those customers coming back. One proven technique is to leak tantalizing suggestions about the product/service, but hold back the details, as speculation leads to buzz.

Tip 3: Deal with customer complaints promptly and decisively

No one likes disappointing a customer, but valid complaints actually aid your business as they tell you what you are doing wrong—and they're unsolicited, to boot. Complaints are much more valuable than compliments; they tell you specifically how you can improve. Customers who give you this sort of feedback are worth rewarding, as they could save you thousands or even millions of dollars. You may consider providing a small token of your appreciation to complaining customers. If you don't, they will be less likely to come back and visit again.

Remember: Better to have your customers complain to you than to have them complain to each other or to your competition. Research indicates unhappy customers tell many more people their impressions than happy ones do. Wouldn't you prefer that they said, "I was really unhappy with the quality of a part, but then the manager gave me a refurbished model that did the trick, so they really do listen." This sort of comment is likely to retain customers and burnish your reputation.

Customer complaints are usually specific, which makes them easier to address. You'll have to follow through to ensure your solution hits the mark, and this gives you your best chance to end that transaction on a high note. The more you respond to customer complaints by fixing the basic organizational or product problems, the less you'll be giving out as compensation, the more customers you will retain, and the more profitable your business will be.

If you can't fix the problem right away, be sure to contact your complainer and let him know your plan for fixing it— then tell him what you did to meet his needs and thank him for working with you patiently. Consider that almost all industries have issues that periodically create valid customer complaints. The perception of how you solve those problems can make or break your image in the marketplace.

Tip 4: Unleash the power of FREE

As they say, you've got to give to get. Put that maxim to work in retaining customers. Everyone likes to get something for nothing.

Most software companies allow prospective users to try their full or a limited version of their product for free for a limited time before requiring them to pay for a license. By the end of the trial, the customer may have gotten so attached to the software that he'll come to see it is his—after all, it's already on his computer, performing tasks he likes. Paying for it at that point becomes perfunctory.

The same goes for upgrades. You can offer upgrades to hardware or software products as a free trial, giving customers the latitude to decide to buy in after they're comfortable with the product. As you produce upgrades and add-ons, you'll see your customers coming back for more. Conveniently, this touches back to tip 1: Know what your customer wants. Use the trial period to gauge your customers' interest in the product and the upgrade. As you refine your sense of what the customer wants, you can produce it and he'll return for it.

The power of FREE can also be applied to service businesses. Provide a quick survey or scaled down version of your service free so your prospect can better understand the value of what you are selling.

Tip 5: Help customers get the most from your product

Concise, clear instructions on how to best use your product or service will help customers get the most out of your product and improve the likelihood they will return. Be sure you test your usage instructions on someone who knows nothing about the product. Give her the product exactly as a customer would receive it in the box. Watch her unpack it, read the instructions (or not), and try to use it. Money invested in good user documentation is always justified.

If you have excellent documentation and you explain to your customers that your gadget will work even better—and why that's the case—with a new add-on, you'll get yourself some returning customers. It all depends on the quality of your communication.

Don't overlook product care. If you touch base with your customer after the purchase to remind her about the product's maintenance schedule, ensuring its long life, she'll come back to you time and again. Who among us hasn't received such reminders from our car dealerships? These mailings keep the dealership's name in front of us, provide a value (the maintenance schedule), and offer useful discounts on oil changes. And while we're in for our tune up, we might check out the parts department and the showroom floor.

When targeting customers of a Web-based product or service, encourage them to sign up for account maintenance, or to verify their account status. When they log in, help them find something else that they like and want to have. Just do this sparingly. Spamming customers will send them lunging for the "unsubscribe" link. Consider employing a telephone sales company to make follow-up calls to check on satisfaction and offer related products or services. Again, do this sparingly! Put yourself in your customer's shoes so you can find the balance between useful contact and annoyance.

Tip 6: Make your product or service "sticky"

Stickiness in customer retention means that you make it hard for the customer to move away from your service. People aren't fond of change to begin with, and they'll put up with a lot if their perceived cost of jumping ship—time, effort, and inconvenience—is greater than the reward of the unknown. "Better the devil you know than the devil you don't." Of course, none of us wants to bedevil our valued customers.

Banking is a classic example of stickiness. Accounts can be a little tricky to establish in the first place, so once customers get one, they tend to stick with it unless they find the service extremely unsatisfying. Once a customer opens an account, he sets up direct deposit for paychecks, and direct payments for bills such as subscriptions, mortgage payments, utilities, revolving credit, and so forth. The average customer, once he's tied up in all this, tends to stay put unless he receives massive service account charges, which can undo all those prior customer acquisition efforts in a heartbeat. In banking, the industry assumption is that if they can get you to sign up for three services, they have you as a customer for life.

So, too, computer operating systems. For years, Apple has worked hard to get Windows users to switch loyalties. It's seldom a slam-dunk, in large part because of stickiness.

Windows users may perceive that "learning Macs" will feel alien or they won't have access to their favorite software. Of course, for its part, Apple is excelling at standardizing its user experience across platforms and across iDevices, flattening the learning curve all the way to the bank.

Brainstorm ways to make your product or service sticky while providing high consumer value, and you'll find ways to keep customers.

We've discussed the value to you in maintaining existing customers, but how long will that customer deliver profitability if he doesn't continue to see a high value in doing business with you? Let's talk about this from both the business and consumer customer viewpoints.

Business customers: These folks compare profits they make on their product or service against the cost of engaging you for your services. You are a cost. When you stop providing enough value, they'll leave. Don't fool yourself into believing that a business can't quantify your value, or isn't rating your worth every so often. Find ways to show how your product or services contributes to the value of your customer's product or service.

I once helped a software company see how customers would quantify the value we provided. We estimated, with reasonable accuracy, how much our software offering added to customers' sales. We did this by leveraging customer general product gross margin information for most of their offerings. This analysis showed that our services ranged from a "great deal" to a "fair deal", and it was only a matter of time before we would lose them—unless the company changed something. So armed, we reviewed our business model and cost structures, and adjusted both our offerings and pricing. I'm pleased to say the client provided more value and reduced customer attrition and churn.

Look at your product or service value under the same microscope, and adjust to keep profitable customers.

Tip 7: Inform your customers

When your customers are steeped in great information about your products, services and story, they'll be more likely to come back for more. Naturally, you'll want to gather their contact information when they purchase from you the first time around so you can stay in touch. Here are a few great methods for keeping clients and customers informed, engaged and on your side:

One of the best ways to do this is still some version of a newsletter. These can be electronic or physical. In fact, many leading companies publish some version of both. Google, Yahoo, and Microsoft, uncontested technology leaders, still produce informative paper and/or electronic mailings.

Whatever the format, use the medium to announce discounts, upcoming sales, product releases, and new services. You can profile customer success stories and tell your story about doing well in the customer's community. If you plan to send newsletters through e-mail, look into a service such as Campaign Monitor, which allows you to include a set number of links through to your website. Doing so lets you track how many customers click on each link and stay with each item, which gives you valuable data on what your customers consider relevant. Focus on more of those things in upcoming issues. Some services show you where the recipients who've clicked are located, giving you deeper insights into customer interest geographically.

Don't just assume that your customers know what you have to offer. Target customers based on their interest, and show them that you can meet their specific needs. Be careful not to wear out your welcome by too-frequent contact or contact that lacks value—you'll have your customers searching for the trash can or the "unsubscribe" link.

Tip 8: Surprise your customers

Surprise your customers with unexpected benefits for a killer retention strategy. Say you're a camera reseller. Once a customer buys a camera from you, maybe a high-end SLR, give him a free camera case or quantity of high-quality print processing as your way of saying thanks.

A surprise gift, in contrast with an incentive, is impressive, touching and flattering, and these customers will return the favor with repeat business. After all, you learned to under-promise and over-perform for a reason. It works. This is another way to unleash the power of FREE.

Tip 9: Develop a customer service culture

Customer service is a core competency for any successful customer retention strategy. A robust customer service focus will help your customers to feel positive about your goods or services. It shows you stand behind your line, care about creating customer value, and value your customers. When shoppers feel that your service is competent, pleasant, and friendly, they'll keep coming back for more.

Very few companies can get away with bad customer service. For example, even banks, which have a high degree of stickiness, have become notorious for hidden fees and shunting consumers away from live tellers and toward ATMs and automated phone banking. Bank of America's debit card price increase led to such negative press, strong consumer pushback, and much-publicized defection to other banks that they had to abandon the new charges.

Once in a great while, bad customer service is part of the charm, as is the case of *Seinfeld's* fictional "soup nazi." In these cases, management seems to take apparent pride in getting customer service all wrong, and patrons return time and again with a new batch of friends in tow to see it for themselves. These successes notwithstanding, poor service is not a staple you want on your menu.

Quick tips to consider when stating your customer relations strategy

- Customer relations approaches and policies should be written down and understood by everyone in the company. Everyone is part of marketing. Everyone is selling all the time.
- Always follow up with clients and customers after their purchase to check that everything went well.
- Set dispute-resolution policies to streamline and quickly act on customer complaints, and monitor their effectiveness.
- Introduce a culture in your business where everyone is considered a customer, particularly the employees. Doing so inspires problem solving, attentiveness, and responsibility: all heart-healthy habits of a successful business.
- Train frontline staff in customer service. Often the customer's first and only contact with your company is with lower-level employees, so you have to take positive steps to ensure they understand this responsibility and know how to respond. This doesn't have to be a great expense; you'll find plenty of help online, including documentation, webinars, and podcasts that explain how to treat customers. You must also hire and retain attentive, bright staff who show they're eager to provide and mentor in top-notch customer service.

Actually, if you run a training course, even if it's only half a day with a lot of follow up reading, you show your employees that you value them, you value customer service, and you want them to value your customers. The sheer fact that a training course is an unusual occurrence means it has a bigger impact than handing out a manual and telling employees that those are the rules.

Tip 10: Manage your supply chain with a customer focus

Customers want to be able to get their hands on your products and services when they need them, or at the very least, when you've promised them. You won't keep customers if you can't deliver on time.

Develop and routinely monitor service level agreements (SLAs) with your suppliers. These set forth when goods shall be delivered, either to you or to the customer. If a supplier cannot meet your SLA requirements, you will need to either move on to a new supplier or renegotiate with your customers. SLAs strip away ambiguity, and they help center relationships throughout the supply chain for stronger, better-managed service.

Effective supply chain management also relies on good demand forecasting. Anticipate your peak sales times, and make sure to have sufficient stock on hand to meet demand. Be careful not to stick yourself with too much inventory, particularly perishable items.

In services, you may run up against capacity limits to what you can provide. Understand what your supplier or distributor can guarantee to avoid overpromising and under delivering, which would disappoint customers. It's best to get it right the first time.

Tip 11: Create discount alliances

Give your customers the benefit of earning discounts when they support businesses you've partnered with, particularly those in related service areas. For example, a hiking club

---

Hammer Out the Deal

How do you get money when you need it? Understand accounting and finance—as well as the consequences of your options and choices. It can make or break you.

Bill was founder and majority owner of a privately-held build-to-suit construction company. He also developed real estate projects of his own, for around half of his total business. Bill, fifty-something, boasted an excellent reputation for work quality, timely delivery, and budget discipline. Unfortunately, he was caught off guard when the economy tanked and market needs changed. As credit dried up and fewer customers were able to secure pre-approved financing, Bill was stuck. Sales spiraled downward. The recession would wipe a lot of people out.

Financing on both the construction and purchaser sides, became key to sales. It was in Bill's best interest to partner with his customers in ways to afford his work. With my help, Bill began partnering with lenders and equity groups that could provide preapproved financing in a changing market.

You might wake up and find you're missing market share. What change must you make to build a stronger business?

---

might offer discounts at an outdoor gear store, and the outdoor gear store would offer discounts at the hiking club. Airlines often let customers apply earned air miles to patronize partners' goods and services, just as those partners reward their shoppers with air miles toward flights. Everybody wins.

It doesn't take much for a customer to perceive he's gained extra value in this situation. Don't feel you have to go overboard in setting the discount: just something measurable. You know your customers; you know what they'll value personally. Alternatively, you might offer something that costs you very little, but is a relative boon to your partner: Consider

Internet advertising: You provide details of a discount to your customers at the other business and they then in turn get free advertising from you. A couple of decent alliances of this nature can help to make your product enticingly sticky for customers, since if they stop frequenting your business, they know they'll lose the advantages you've made it possible for them to enjoy elsewhere.

Tip 12: Remember your customer's special events

Finally, find a way to focus on the special events in your customers' lives, such as birthdays, Father's Day, Mother's Day, graduations, and the like. What better time to remind customers that you're standing by to help them make a strong connection where it counts? Position your service or product as a thoughtful gift your customer might bestow on friends or family.

Succeeding at this requires that you build a system to remind the customer of these pending events, and allow lead time for shipping. For example, if you are in the business of chocolate gifts ordered online, you know when, why, and likely for whom a customer has been buying your product. Remind him or her that it's that happy time again, and you recommend this, that, or the other thing—with a five percent discount for purchase within the next 24 hours. These are the crucial warm or hot leads your sales team craves.

If you can afford it, send your client and customers a card or small token of appreciation on their special days—say, a discount on one of your goods or services, or a special deal on a partner's offerings. Some companies do this exceedingly well. Brooks Brothers just sent me a Black Friday special e-mail offering the lowest price I have ever seen on their wrinkle-free shirts. I really hadn't considered buying new shirts until that e-mail arrived.

This is just as applicable to business customers as to consumer customers – the decision-makers in a business are individuals, not departments! Focus attention on the special events in the lives of those decision-makers and make a small gesture that lets them know you think of them as individuals. For example send them a birthday card. Let everyone else send them a holiday card.

***

Recap

There's extra money on the table, and it's within marketing's grasp. How many of these 12 tips for defining products, creating leads and retaining customers are you putting to work?

Tip 1: Know What Your Customers Want

Tip 2: Create Anticipation for New Products

Tip 3: Deal with customer complaints promptly and decisively.

Tip 4: Unleash the power of FREE.

Tip 5: Help customers get the most from your product.

Tip 6: Make your product or service "sticky."

Tip 7: Inform your customers.

Tip 8: Surprise your customers.

Tip 9 Develop a customer service culture.

Tip 10: Manage your supply chain with a customer focus.

Tip 11: Create discount alliances.

Tip 12: Remember your customer's special events.

****

Remember, most functional areas could do a much better job communicating with their peers in other areas. The summaries below suggest one tip each peer noted below will normally like to talk to marketing about, and five bedrock tips to use where you see the most value.

Tips to Better Communicate With the:

Board – Tip 1: Know what your customers want.

CEO – Tip 2: Create anticipation for new products.

CFO – Tip 6: Make your product or service "sticky."

COO – Tip 10: Manage your supply chain with your customer in mind.

CMO/CSO – Tip 12: Remember your customer's special events.

CTO/ CIO – Tip 7: Inform your customers.

CPO/SVP-HR – Tip 5: Help customers get the most from your product.

Frank Leadership Tips

Tip 4: Unleash the power of free.

Tip 8: Surprise your customers.

Tip 9: Develop a customer service culture.

Tip 11: Create discount alliances.

Tip 12: Remember your customer's special events.

Strategic conversations

Whenever marketing engages with leadership on such strategic issues, weigh the thrust of the issue against these listener concerns:

I need to know!

I don't know

Why won't you tell me?

How can you tell me?

Help them fill in the blanks. Help your business sell more, provide higher customer value, attract and retain top talent, account for profits and losses and lead its industry.

Strategy on applying the issues you see through this process:

When you see a blind spot opportunity or risk, ask yourself all three of these concerns?

1. Do I have the courage to do something about this?
2. Do I have the passion to do it even though it is impossible to do?
3. Am I willing to share the glory to get this solved?

Coming up: So you think you "get" your sales department? Without meaning to, these dedicated workers may be hiding millions from you. To help uncover that money, let's put sales under a friendly microscope.

Chapter 4

Understanding Millions in Sales: What Sales May Not Be Telling You

In chapters two and three we talked about how marketing helps us decide on the product offering. Now that we have a customer's active interest, let's close the sale. After all, without growing topline sales profitably, where's the growth to create opportunities in operations, human resources, technical, administrative, and executive departments?

Do you know what drives a successful sales department? Do you know the secrets your sales team knows, and how to leverage that knowledge for extra profit? Training, modernization, skills development for your sales people. The old dogs might bristle at some of this, but the young pups live it with their digital, always-on devices and communities. As a leader, where do you want individual contributors, and where do you want more collaborative actions? Sales people are competitive. Recognize it. Encourage it. Reward it.

Let's walk through sales' turf and get you up to speed on several key concepts and practices including a different, strategic way to drive extra millions of revenue growth to accelerate scaling your business. Experienced salespeople, use this chapter to consider how you can help break down functional silos and keep the entire team informed, enlightened, and singing your praises.

Just as everyone in your company is in marketing, everyone in your company is in sales. Maybe not explicitly, but certainly potentially. Everyone is plugged into social media and online marketing; everyone is familiar with what's possible in customer relations management, or will be. Let's look at how to leverage this at your businesses.

In Chapter 5, I'll help you master sales tactics to uncover those missing millions beyond insurance.

It's All About Connection

With more consumer choices offered every day and buyers overturning traditional marketing channels for social media experiences, it's more important than ever to nurture customer relations and put buyers to work touting your message and brand. But how do you professional service firms and small business owners win customers' attention, action, and loyalty? How do such firms avoid pestering clients? How do they get the maximum return with minimum overhead?

Oh, for the good old days, veterans might lament. "Why, I remember when I could put in a call or send out a card, and I'd know that my client would take the time to respond." Salespeople used to refer to this customer contact as the doughnut run. The sales rep would schedule regular visits to established customers and be welcomed with professional courtesy and genuine warmth. Coca-Cola was famous for it, so were Marlboro, Xerox and a host of others. Even your life insurance salesman would call you on your birthday.

The good old days are gone, and not necessarily for the better. These days, with always-on broadband technology, we edit out nonproductive, invasive, and especially unsolicited communiqués. We spend more time binning e-mail than we do reading it, and no sales organization worth its salt will tolerate anything less from its reps than "optimal lead conversion." We've thrown the doughnut run overboard in the name of productivity. That's unfortunate.

Twitter—which has taken the world by storm in packets of 140 characters times billions—is a perfect illustration of the frenetic pace of Internet-based social networking and communications technology. Twitter has its uses, but is rightly criticized as a media darling: novel, yes, but certainly neither inevitable nor irreplaceable. I think Twitter is making waves, and we're right to ride it while it's here, but too many salespeople are using it as a crutch. They have no idea how to send a stronger message that gets results.

Pin your business success on the basics: no matter what the demographic, sound marketing based on creating clear customer value will always drive successful business-to-business relationships.

Tap Tough-Times Opportunities

In business and in professional services, we hunger for reliable information. Not for trivia, mind you; but for genuine, researched, actionable information. Consider this: as circulation of mass daily newspapers such as *The Daily Telegraph* (UK) has plunged, circulation of the authoritative *Wall Street Journal* has surged. The paper appeals to financial-market watchers, yes, but we also see that the *Journal* appeals increasingly to people in business seeking authoritative, genuine, useful, corroborated news and views.

If you see yourself as a professional, and want to offer value to your clients and customers, put yourself in front of them at every opportunity. But do so methodically, strategically, and genuinely. Whether they are clients, prospects, or introducers, people who stay close to their contacts will enjoy success—particularly in tough times.

It's easier than ever to make and maintain that closeness. Look beyond Twitter and Facebook. You've got the telephone, e-mail, shared articles, or white papers. You've got greeting cards and postcards. You've got video clips. You've got books and articles you can recommend with authority thereby making a personal connection that provides value.

Are you using these classic "touches" to best effect? Are you asking your customer how he's traveling in these troubled times? Are you sending e-mails marking customer birthdays, business launch anniversaries, and new market initiatives? Are you sending postcards from a trip? "Old-fashioned" yet fundamental touch points give a relationship depth and texture. They're remembered and appreciated.

Be on the lookout for opportunities to "touch" contacts and demonstrate your expertise. Even a change to legislation gives you an occasion to reach out to contacts. And if you have subject matter expertise, use it. Put together a white paper and other marketing initiatives. If you lack the time or inclination to do that, snip and mail articles of interest to select clients. Make sure to attach a brief, friendly note: "Thought you might like to see this."

We live in an age of massive turmoil. Your contacts will appreciate your genuine, grounding interest.

How well have you considered the impact of stories like how one smart ad agency that wanted to convey the theme "big ideas, small budget," sent out cards the size of postage stamps instead of its traditional Christmas cards? It got its message out perfectly.

Measure Return on Effort

Also known as return on investment (ROI), your return on effort is the result: the revenues, the profits after marketing expenses (including promotion expenses, agency fees, and event management fees for product launches). Your aim, after all is to make money, right? Remember: When you spend your time on social media outlets such as Twitter, Facebook, and Pinterest, it's all about return on effort. Use your time to pack a punch.

The challenge is to quantify the value of leads and sales that you generate from marketing and sales campaigns. The calculation is not simply the next sale to a customer: Rather, it is the lifetime value of the customer. This is the amount of revenue that one customer will generate over the life of the relationship, whether you measure it in weeks or years.

Say you're a mobile phone service provider. You know that the average customer spends $100 a month on your service. As calculated over the full 12 months, your customer pays $1,200. Let's say that customer stays with you for three and a half years. The revenue you generate from the customer over that period is $4,200 ($100/month x 12 months x 3.5 years).

Naturally, there will be a cost for you to service that customer—let's say $30 per month. The total cost to service them over the full term of their time as your customer is $1,260. ($30 per month for 12 months over three and a half years.)

Therefore, a customer lifetime value would be the equivalent revenue generated by that customer over the term, which in this illustration is 3.5 years. This equates to $4,200, less the cost of serving that customer over the 3.5 years, resulting in $2,940. Now, say the cost of acquiring that customer is 10 percent of customer lifetime value: the amount spent is approximately $294. This could be assessed as the marketing costs to gain a new customer.

In some textbooks, this is called cost per acquisition, or cost per sale. The formula is useful in setting marketing campaign metrics and arming management and other decision-makers with key performance indicators toward assessing marketing plans and campaigns.

We generally accept that it costs up to five times as much to win a new customer as it does to retain an established customer. Our math above bears this out, and this is why most businesses spend time and money to retain customers. It almost always pays to keep existing customers happy.

Generate Leads

Selling products over the Internet, though not the same as serving a customer in a brick and mortar store, is nonetheless a relationship. After all, large-volume digital marketers such as iTunes Music Store and Amazon.com have earned impressive customer retention rates. But even these folks, just like Main Street plumbing contractors, business coaches and Realtors, need to generate leads.

Online and offline, lead generation begins with a prospect who might show some interest in your product or service. If you think of lead generation as a kind of sales funnel, then your task is to convert that prospect into a customer.

As I showed above, the only thing that really counts toward successful ROI is cost of your effort against the lifetime value of a customer. Therefore, you must determine your lead's value.

The calculation is simple: assess the number of leads generated over a given period and divide that by the number of new customers generated from those leads. If, for example, you produce 300 leads and 100 sales over the previous 12 months, then the lead conversion rate is 100/300, or 30 percent. Going back to the lifetime value: if this value is $1,000 then a lead is worth 30 percent of $1,000, or $300. Hence, each lead generated from your marketing effort is worth $300 to you.

Use Your Time Wisely

Time is indeed a scarce commodity. Most small business leaders juggle many urgent priorities, and the cost for dropping a ball is high. This is an example of the value or cost of not maximizing a salesperson's time in front of qualified prospects. Sales and marketing experts often talk about measuring how much time sales spends face-to-face or belly-to-belly with customers. That personal interaction in most industries is still the best way for salespersons to sell more.

Another excellent use of your time: investing in ongoing sales training. As a rule of thumb, fewer than 60 percent of salespeople meet quota, and the win rate of forecasted deals falls beneath 50 percent. Moreover, 60 percent of salespeople ask for more training. Train your people. (Years ago, I invested in sales champ Tom Hopkins' three-day Boot Camp Sales Mastery, because I felt unsupported and inadequately trained. It made a world of difference.)

If sales struggles so to meet quota, and if the win rate on sales funnel targets is so low, the pressure is going to radiate throughout the organization to attain corporate sales and profitability targets.

If you're not going to sell effectively, why are you in business? Where is your front-line point of sales staff undertrained and poorly supported? That's your blind spot.

Lead Generation and Social Media

Increasingly, customers—or potential customers—turn to each other via the Internet to gather opinions about you, your product or service, and your competitors. You need to be part of that conversation. You want to connect with people looking for what you offer and meet them in their own space.

Treat your investment in social media—Twitter, Facebook, Foursquare, Pinterest and the like—the same as you would any marketing campaign, paying careful attention to return on effort. Do your staff and paid agencies know what constitutes acceptable return? Make sure they know, or they'll be spinning their wheels.

Naturally, you will have to invest relatively heavily in social media to penetrate teen and young adult markets, as that's the only place such consumers go to get news and views— and increasingly, to develop ideas for things to buy and places to travel.

Contrast that with the B2B space, where you can get away with a considerably smaller social media spend. LinkedIn, the leading professional networking site, is a good tool to use to keep ties fresh, solicit or bestow introductions, and research allies and applicants. Its popularity is on the rise.

Similarly, even at the professional services level (think accounting and business coaching), Twitter is useful in positioning yourself as an expert and part of the conversation. And because users judge you on the usefulness of your posts and reposts and by the quality of the people you follow and who follow you, you will score points by just being yourself: involved, connected and sincere. But make sure you justify that investment with solid results. Set metrics to manage your time. Messaging at random because it's fun or because it feels like a customer relations process is neither sustainable nor justifiable. Make sure each action you take supports a stated marketing strategy and drives desired gains in sales revenue and bottom-line profit.

Even creating and maintaining a blog has to earn its keep. Business is not a vanity game; it's about generating leads, sales and profits. Even if your idea is to position yourself as an expert, justify your actions purely from the hard-nosed perspective of return on effort.

Keep in Touch—and Grow

Consider that bigger, better, and more profitable in a controllable environment is often viewed by most business people with enthusiasm on par with motherhood and apple pie. When companies fully appreciate marketing, the department's input directly supports the business growth strategy, which you may be familiar with as "high growth" and "scaling." I call it survival. Without profitable growth and satisfied customers, where will you find the funds to create new jobs, justify promotions, and allow fatter incentive checks?

With that in mind, we can lay out the framework for growth throughout your company:

In the digital age, staying in touch and deepening customer relationships is essential to growth. Take a page from the big boys: entrepreneurs and Internet hopefuls often cite luminaries such as Apple's iTunes Music Store, Amazon.com, and Facebook as examples of perfectly scalable business models. Certainly, if you want to build a business that has impact, then at some point you have to scale. Even if a business idea takes root in a dorm room or parents' garage, the business proper is built by deep, layered, and committed teams of people.

Google, arguably the definitive 'Net superstar, employs 20,000. Facebook boasts more than 1,500. Whatever the size of your business or the size of your business after accomplishing your present goals and dreams, consider that business owners who have successfully scaled up--or tried and fell short—agree:

- Business owners who are determined to scale need a mentor.
- Some seasoned executives on your team are key to success.

- Team members must collaborate toward a shared vision.
- Scaling businesses requires systems and processes to ensure communication and accountability.

Growth is tremendously exciting. Just having an idea worth building a business around is an accomplishment most people will never enjoy. But scaling is a skill set even fewer people share, as it comes from experience. How would a business owner know... well, what he doesn't know? That's why it's common sense and practical wisdom to choose seasoned mentors and experienced employees, while developing your own track record in the art and science of scaling.

Get Ready for Change and Let Sales Lead the Way

Growing businesses often report that communication, even basic communication among employees, is a surprising challenge. What worked well for the first few years, with scale now seems to miss the mark. But it's the same way we've always done it. What's wrong?

Process management experts counsel that businesses need to build in efficient communication for success. As we scale up, the cost in noise and poorly encoded or decoded messages is magnified as a function of the number of people involved. A business of five people hardly needs process, as they can just talk to each other. Hundreds or thousands of people? Now you need technology. Now you need to collaborate.

One key point is to monitor the basis of competition. Do you sell at best price? Highest quality? Fastest delivery? Best finance terms? Greatest innovation? Reputation? Service? Support? Marketing normally gets that right and sales executes accordingly, but business climates are fickle. Good sales people in the field with customers are most likely to be the first people to feel the shifting of the wind, and balance approaches as needed. With less customer face-time, marketing might not pick up on the change as rapidly as it should. Consider how well your organization communicates and responds to this cutting edge market information to better manage this potential blind spot.

Scaling a business mostly relates to how effectively you leverage communications technology. You'll be rewarded for identifying tasks, spelling out everyone's role and accountability, and defining how mission-critical information is passed from person to person, department to executive. At this scale, effective communication actually becomes trickier. Your solution is a robust communications process built to handle the load, eliminate uncertainty, and protect against costly blind spots.

Perfect and Expand the Prototype

Here's an example from my files. Restaurant owners can mint money when pleasant employees deliver high-quality, consistently prepared food quickly under a well thought-out system. Reduce that quality, aggravate the customer, slow down delivery time, or fail to maintain clean bathrooms, and disaster overwhelms that same restaurant.

Not in the restaurant business? The logic applies to you too. I've seen high-growth and disaster scenarios played out in companies ranging from small fast-food joints to cutting-edge high-tech leaders.

In the hamburger business, when we smiled and said thank you, delivered a consistently high-quality product, and quickly got cash to the bank, we thrived. When competitors failed to execute similar tactics, they lost their shirt. Simple enough to transfer that winning recipe to the building products industry, where I suggested a Fortune 500 client in steel's international division apply the same basic marketing and scaling solutions. They work.

Just Enough Chefs in the Kitchen

Address skepticism before it addresses you. To operate at full strength, you need a team united behind your vision, your mission, and your values. Even if you're uncomfortable to admit that changes are needed in your business model or execution, let them know what's going on. The worst thing that can happen to you in business is unchecked internal strife.

Joe, a forty-something restaurant developer serving up his third success, was having a sweet time. His expertise was in building a company, making it profitable, selling it, and paying his investors big profits. Unfortunately, (there's too often an "unfortunately," isn't there?) the company lost a key profitable partnership, and found itself depending on a newer, riskier, less financeable restaurant concept. Joe needed three times the equity original estimates called for.

Joe learned in a flash that financial sources and partners hate to be blindsided with bad financial news, particularly when they learn about a series of bad fiscal decisions only after the fact. Understandably, Joe's investors were now worried whether he could deliver big projected profits. The heat was on.

Joe and his team had been missing reliable, forward-looking financial information and projections. When I looked at the program, as investors fumed, I served Joe two options: continue the original plan, but triple the intended investment or accept a structured approach to developing a more geographically focused area for his offerings.

He chose the latter. It worked, of course. Confidence restored.

The hamburger success story, of course, comes with a lesson on sales and scaling from Ray Kroc, who led McDonald's restaurants from humble beginnings to a global juggernaut.

After taking over what was in 1954 a small and uneven chain of restaurants, Ray Kroc perfected, to the last detail, his vision for the way McDonald's restaurant would run. By 1961, his commitment to standardization of operations and quality allowed him to replicate his success—thousands and thousands of times over. (For an interesting article on the origins of hamburgers up to and including the McDonald's chain, check out http://health.learninginfo.org/hamburger.htm.) Kroc needed not just standardized systems and procedures, but informed and trained employees backed by a unified organizational structure. If McDonald's was going to thrive, Kroc needed to find others to do the line work. And he found them. Kroc prepared employees to handle the technical details—both manual and managerial—and freed himself for strategic thinking.

For businesspeople planning to grow beyond their personal management style or limitations, Kroc's concept is clarity personified.

Of course, Kroc's approach is hardly restricted to food retail. Virtually any business case can apply it. An effective proto-type is more than a well-oiled machine, it's a business that finds and keeps customers—profitably—better than any other competitor.

Turn the Key

Here's what Kroc really built, and what you can master too: turnkey systems.

When you buy a new car, you don't have to open the hood and fiddle with the engine. You just strap in, turn the key, and hit the road. In business, a turnkey is a system so finely crafted that it's good to go right off the lot. No debugging, fiddling, or head scratching required. Just open the door and start making money. If your business is starting to feel more like a rut

QUESTIONS & ANSWERS

GREG WHITE |
CEO, Blue Ridge Inventory Group
MARIETTA, GA.

Greg White says he loves making his living helping companies make millions by improving the way they manage their inventory. Backed by decades of experience managing inventory and merchandising, he and his companies help optimize demand fulfillment and inventory investment for retailers and distributors of every size, from Fortune 500 customers to "a guy who sells gloves out of his garage."

Blue Ridge employs approximately thirty people and boasts $5 million to $7 million in revenue.

Gary Patterson: Greg, you seem to thrive as a big-picture guy who excels at mastering processes down at the granular level. As an executive, how sure are you that you are asking your own people the right questions so that you have the big picture at your companies?

Greg White: I make it a personal goal to ask the proper questions to get a clear picture from my folks. My questions are probing, and I either get the answer or continue digging until I have the necessary information—or realize the person I'm asking can't give me the answer.

GP: Whose responsibility is it to set this tone?

GW: I'm a borderline micromanager. I try to set the direction for people. Paul Rose, a wise man [and vice president corporate inventory at Henry Schein, Inc.] once told me, "You don't get what you expect; you get what you inspect." What are we doing as a team? What are the gotchas?

The burden is on your board members, your execs. You have to be diligent. You get what you inspect. I measure everything. When Paul Rose is hit by a gotcha, he fixes it. And fixing it to him starts with asking the question, "What can I have done ten steps back to have prevented this from happening?"

GP: Are your people sharing the right information with each other and you?

GW: Most often, we are sharing the right information, but not always complete information. That usually comes down to whether we're listening, or just waiting to jump in and talk.

GP: What, in your opinion, is the right information?

GW: The right information for me is that which allows me to assess the situation and make a decision or assessment on the spot. My day is full of so many evaluations—I couldn't have contemplated how many before being a CEO—and I always try to remember that my people can't even begin to imagine how many decisions and evaluations I make in a day. I recognize that it is my responsibility to extract concise, complete, and correct information from the team, and I strive to make that my burden.

GP: How well would you say your leadership team is empowered to fight blind spots?

GW: Some are more empowered than others. I believe you have people who are more discerning than others. Ultimately, it comes down to my trust of their capability to effectively assess and deliver information.

GP: How do you want to be told information that the deliverer might be reluctant to share?

GW: I want to hear what the issue is and what solution he suggests. Further, I'd like to know what priority he put on it. I often ask, "Would you put this higher or lower on the priority list than X?" This also helps them gain perspective on the relative importance of the issue. Otherwise, if people only think about the count of issues, I find you will have people worried that things are crumbling around them. Perspective is key.

A problem without a solution is a complaint. We're not about complaining, we're about solving problems. I don't care if it's a dumb solution. If you're presenting a problem, present it to me as an opportunity: "Here's how I see us fixing it, capitalizing on it."

Some people think in very structured, linear, and singular ways. I'll ask, "What are our options? Why couldn't we do it another way? Why couldn't we do it this way?" That gets people thinking. Sometimes I'll have the option; sometimes I won't.

In addition to being CEO at Blue Ridge Inventory, Greg is chairman and CEO at Exactorder, which helps clients eliminate stockouts without breaking the bank; is chairman of Intrinsic Value Chain Solutions, a holding company for supply chain technology ventures; and past director of professional services at Servigistics and leader of On-demand solutions at E3 Corporation.

than a business, then it is time for you to find a new way of doing business: the turnkey approach. A turnkey system is any method or procedure that simplifies or automates part of the business, making it easier for ordinary people to operate.

Work on Your Attitude

This is the essence of what entrepreneur guru and *The E-Myth* author Michael Gerber calls the prototype. Gerber talks often about how 80 percent of businesses fail in the first five years. He reports that most people become sick of working for their "idiot bosses," so they decide to start their own businesses—and end up becoming the idiot boss. Instead of working five days per week for guaranteed pay, they now get to work six to seven days per week, often for no pay. Do you relate to those sad statistics?

In his follow-up, *The E-Myth Revisited*, Gerber walks a business owner through various stages of a business life cycle to highlight the points of inflection for success and failure. He famously asserts a major distinction: working *on* your business versus working *in* your business. To grow a business, he says; focus on freedom, not servitude. Do you work for your business, or does your business work for you? Michael Gerber has a company website with more information about him and his blog at   http://www.michaelegerbercompanies.com/

A true business is a profitable enterprise that thrives without you, and rewards you with passive income. Most people who believe they have a business really only have a job, one that concentrates incredible stress and liability on the owner. Could you go sailing for six months and know that your business is thriving? Most people do not know how to set up a business like that. They just have jobs.

Just as McDonald's restaurants are replicated tens of thousands of times over around the world, your business can run itself on a turnkey basis if you set up the right systems and procedures.

For a manager, the systems approach provides vital order and predictability. For a proficient technical specialist or professional business operator-owner, it allows others to do the heavy lifting. Why shouldn't you be free to focus on strategy, go sailing, spend more time on charitable works, or start additional successful businesses?

Every business has its own unique characteristics. Your task as the business owner is to identify and build your own appropriate, systems, written as a procedures and tasks manual (sometimes called operations manuals). Every segment of your business has procedures that constitute your workflow, consistent with set strategic goals and corporate values.

Just because you're armed with a business plan or a set of strategic goals hardly means running your business will be any easier. You've got to perfect your systems, procedures, and organizational structure. Ray Kroc sweated over this before he *knew* that a franchise operator could come in, switch on the lights, and deliver the same high-quality hamburger time and time again. He handled, examined, improved, and documented every detail of the business, and now that business is an icon.

Say you've earned some experience making sales, negotiating with suppliers, and tracking expenses. At some point, you're going to realize that either (a) this is as far as you believe you can go, or (b) there's a lot more value you can create for yourself and clients. At that point, you need to scale up: penetrate new markets, take on a region, a niche or an industry, and delve into systems and procedures.

Now you need to leverage technology to "touch" your contacts, highlight your expertise, and deepen your relationships. Now you must quantify the cost of your sales and marketing efforts, and fix the financial value of your leads and customers. When appropriate, you can tap social media to reach and connect with leads and customers profitably.

If a business owner wants to scale her business with the least overhead, she would be well advised to seek out a mentor, hire experienced personnel, and enhance collaboration through the development of turnkey systems, which would ensure proper expectations and accountability.

This investment requires buy-in from all key people. Ask yourself: what would best serve our customers? How could we streamline our practices to create the greatest customer value with the least overhead? How can we set this up so that it runs on its own power, freeing us up to think strategically and meet new goals?

Now you're in business.

To help build that business and exploit those missing millions in sales, the next chapter provides a dozen secret tips: focused tactics to ensure you exploit the full benefits that marketing can provide all areas of the business.

***

Bedrock truths:

Time in front of the customer is key.

Process and procedures are the keys to scale and growth.

Measure return on efforts.

Generate leads.

Keep in touch.

Keep your customers.

Chapter 5

Uncover Millions in Sales

If you fail to effectively market and sell your products or services, then you won't make money and you'll be out of business. The market will close around you as if you were never there. Here's where you need all hands on deck to anticipate, prevent, and deal with risk. Do you approach sales and marketing with discipline, targeting desired outcomes, or do these activities feel like hopeful shots in the dark?

Be warned. Depending upon your experience with sales and marketing, some of these tips may sound familiar, and you might be tempted to scan, and not critically consider, these issues. But it's in that failure to pay attention, in overfamiliarity, where blind spots multiply. If you "know" these concepts, but don't practice them, what good are they?

Knowledge is power. Take control. Here are 12 secret tips for improving your return on effort in sales and marketing:

Tip 1: Use the sales funnel

Best practices and processes drive sales, just as they do for all functional areas and industries. Don't let that put you off, embrace it. By the end of this section, you'll be prepared to account for buyers' and sellers' risks, move along the sales path confidently, rapidly, and efficiently, and haul in bigger deals to boot. This process is clearly quantifiable, so you can measure your success and build on achievable goals. We call it the sales funnel.

These are the components of the sales funnel:

1. **Initial contact.** The sales team makes initial contact with a prospective client to gauge need or interest in a product or service.
2. **Application of initial fit criteria.** Both sides assess the fit.
3. **Sales lead.** Does the fit appear strong? If so, the client or customer becomes a sales lead for you to pursue.
4. **Needs identification.** Buyer and seller determine whether buyer actually needs the seller's product or service.
5. **Qualified prospect.** If buyer and seller agree on need, then the buyer becomes a qualified prospect.
6. **Proposal.** Seller proposes a sale for the potential buyer to review.
7. **Negotiation.** Buyer and seller come together on price and terms.
8. **Closing.** Buyer and seller reach the final stages of the negotiation, and strike a deal.
9. **Deal transaction.** The deal takes place.

Companies may vary the details, but the sales funnel's structure and goals are common: to close more and larger sales faster. The funnel builds the sales team's work to ensure that everything is handled effectively, and can even be converted into your own best practices to ensure processes are followed as planned.

Don't let sales apply their sales funnel process arbitrarily. All the other areas of the business plan their processes and activities around the dates and sales volume that are collected in this funnel, so it all begins here. Accurate numbers and their strategic impact are crucial:

- Manufacturing uses those projections to schedule its operations.
- HR uses those projections to anticipate hiring needs.
- Finance uses those projections to update estimate cash-flow projections and to track how the organization fares on reaching strategic plans.

A Hard Look at Soft Orders

Don't oversell your product.

Even big companies have problems, and when they screw up, they really screw up. You've heard the adage, "Those who cannot remember the past are condemned to repeat it." Learn from your mistakes, and the mistakes of others.

Remember Cisco's $2.25 billion Q3 2001 inventory write-off? They had state-of-the-art accounting and reporting systems on sales pipelines and backlog, and could deliver volumes of information in days. What were they missing? Red-hot sales had depleted inventories; customers ordered product in excess quantities, just to make sure they got the smaller volume they really needed. But as the market cooled, orders evaporated. It's simple supply and demand. When you gear your supply chain to meet those soft orders, you risk massive corrections.

Cisco didn't understand who their ultimate customers were, and missed focusing on them. Cisco lost nearly $2.5 billion before it managed to balance production to real orders.

Think about the ultimate customer. Cisco didn't. When you focus on your ultimate customer, your sales continue, you're focused, and you won't miss a beat.

What product or service are you ramping up for, based on your sales funnel? Demand could evaporate. What are you missing?

This reminds me of a story that you'll find useful. One CEO, concerned that she saw sales totals move back monthly for several months, tasked me to audit the sales funnel with her head of sales. She told me she didn't care how optimistic or pessimistic my audit determined that the detail listing of sales leads was; she just wanted to be able to rely on the beginning point of sales prospects using a process that her team could trust.

So the head of sales and I scrubbed the pipeline. We tracked down answers to these essential questions:

- Are salespeople merely trumpeting the same prospect each month, and simply moving the expected closing date along to match?
- What else might account for projected closing dates that slid away month to month to month, and what could we do about it?
- Where could we identify a pattern in failing to meet projected delivery dates for closed sales?

What we learned from this process moved us closer to industry best practices that were applied at almost no incremental cost. Best of all, our scrubbed pipeline suddenly became much more reliable for all the other functional areas to use for their planning and operations. Blind spot solved. Don't let your CEO lose faith in you and have to bring in the CFO to audit your sales funnel.

Tip 2: Measure sales team with a "hit rate"
The hit reveals the sales team's effectiveness:

$$\frac{\text{Total Sales Won}}{\text{Total Sales Won} + \text{Total Sales Lost} + \text{Total Sales Abandoned}}$$

The "hit rate" is the percentage obtained by dividing sales won by *sales won, lost, and abandoned*. It lets you set targets to push the sales team to better performance, if possible. You can set metrics for dollars or number of deals. This tool is valuable as a benchmark and can be used to compare individuals within a sales team, and set hit rates for different sales teams or personnel.

It may also be used to compare your company with competitors, though in some cases you may lack access to the relevant figures. The process rewards rigor (read accurate records), but the hit rate is an excellent tool for demonstrating sales effectiveness. Combine this with an ongoing effort to know how sales were lost or abandoned and you will be able to develop training, processes, and best practices to fully use this information.

Tip 3: Sell solutions

Solution selling focuses on putting sales effort into understanding the customer's needs and crafting solutions that fit—not just pushing off-the-shelf goods and services. If you make the customer's problem go away, you've nailed it. You can implement this system through a consultative stage in your sales process, so that your salespeople are free to determine customers' outstanding issues. Make sure your solution provides dramatic, measurable improvement.

Solution selling homes in on need, and is a powerful technique in retaining customers—which, as I've shown, improves your bottom line. Customers aren't always motivated by pain relief; they may just want to purchase an enhancement. Listen to what your customer is saying to determine what she needs, not what the initial want description suggests. You might otherwise pass up a good deal for everyone involved. Be sure to include plenty of proof points such as ROI models, similar case studies, references, and testimonials.

Tip 4: Apply "guided selling"

Here we focus not on customer pain, but on helping customers choose products and services that best meet their needs and helping them to arrive at a buying decision. It's called guided selling and its goal is to increase the seller's conversion rates while also better meeting customer needs

A key element in this process is online automation: taking information a customer provides, considering their needs, and creating a solution that generates a proposal. You'll see this at work online, for example, in personal computer sales. The seller devises a form-based approach by asking users what sort of processor, how much memory they need, and what software they want preinstalled. Then the seller presents a proposal that includes price and delivery.

Now the customer knows exactly what solutions the seller has to offer, and will weigh his or her options and try out alternatives. If the seller's process is earning its keep, it'll track the buyer's choices and refine its proposal on the fly.

You can implement this process for many types of products, especially when products can be customized. These solutions are usually most applicable for online stores, product manufacturing websites, and providers of services where different levels apply to the service. You can also set up call center software in this way to help an agent determine customer need and sell more effectively.

Another benefit for other areas of the business occurs because this information is loaded into your information technology systems. So consider savings for areas including your supply chain and inventory control when you evaluate implementing or upgrading guided selling processes.

Guiding customers to solutions is effective, and worth analyzing the investment in software. Don't let this opportunity slide.

Tip 5: Encourage upselling and cross selling

Upselling and cross selling help strengthen your products and services' value to customers. Look at what your "standard" customer wants or needs. Then you'll know where to guide him, maximizing his return on his investment in you.

Upselling generates a sale that is a greater cost to the customer. Here, your salesperson demonstrates better options available for purchase than the customer perhaps knew existed, or perhaps knew he needed. You're boosting profitability into the sale—more than the original sale may have generated on its own. Think upgrades and add-ons. The salesperson might demonstrate to a customer that your product or service will serve him better with just the right accessory.

Cross selling is a familiar concept, particularly online. We pitch this as, "Most customers who bought X also bought Y." For example, most customers who bought this political thriller also bought a similar series of books from a different author. It shows customers what's nearby on the shelf, if you will.

Think about leveraging these concepts to create additional value for customers and your bottom line. Unless you offer one basic product, or one simple service, you're usually sitting on opportunities for upselling and cross selling. If you're stocked with just a basic product or service, why not add an extended warranty at a modest cost? This will push more profit into your sales.

Tip 6: Implement sales work force management

Here we consider sales force automation (SFA) as opposed to customer relationship management systems (see the next tip). These two systems are interrelated. In some companies, they may even be the same system. Though both approaches are strong, effective, and in popular use, many businesses I've seen apparently have not received the memo. Let sales work-force management no longer be a secret.

First, sales force management systems: these are computer programs that provide a level of automation to business tasks such as sales forecasts and performance, and analyze levels of demand. In the case of a product-based business, they may also track inventory. Sales force management systems usually track all stages in the sales process, and detail all customer contacts with outcomes.

You can even tie sales workforce management into "Tip 1: Use the 'sales funnel'" to ensure your carefully engineered process is automated for even greater return on sales effort. You can store information about specific products in one of the systems mentioned below to ensure that all data required to make the sale are kept together—a one-stop shop for the busy salesperson. Now that's efficient!

In fact, *CRM* magazine specializes on this overall topic and creates annual best-of-breed rankings and research. Use it as your starting point: www.destinationcrm.com. Each year *CRM* recognizes companies' performance with their Market Leader Awards. According to their website, they "rate the top five vendors in 10 categories based on a composite score that includes revenue, revenue growth, market share, customer wins, reputation for customer satisfaction, depth of product functionality and company direction." *CRM magazine's* 2011 winner in the "Sales Force Automation" category space Salesforce.com. The runners-up included Microsoft, Sugar CRM, and NetSuite.

Readers may value www.businessbuyguide.co.uk, which "matches buyers with suppliers across 105 general business categories such as technology, marketing and business services." Consider using this in conjunction with applying "Tip 4: Apply guided selling," in a high-tech setting.

Don't get carried away with using this available information until you have conducted a needs analysis based on your customers, users, unique situations (pre-sales, manufacturing ,or support issues), and you've evaluated whether your present process meets best standards or is past its prime.

There's a reason people still cite GIGO (garbage in, garbage out): IT conversions work best when the organization decides what it needs most to move ahead strategically, and honestly evaluates what changes it needs in its processes and procedures (regardless of size, factor in potential impact of software on demand and the cloud). Without thoughtful, strategic inputs, the output is, well, garbage. Conversions are expensive, intrusive, and disruptive. No one wants to go see their conversion investment rendered obsolete by poor technology choices just as it's getting off the ground, then have to go through the process all over again. Debugging and training add up. Better to get it right the first time.

Consider these three common business situations. Which one of these best describes you?

A. You recently completed a business process re-engineering review and are considering changes—an upgrade, perhaps—to lengthen your lead over the competition. With your access to financial and personnel expertise, you can undertake a major strategic initiative that will boost efficiency and cost effectiveness across your entire business.

B. You have champagne tastes and a beer budget. You need to put a Band-Aid on current processes and find a way to earn or finance your way to upgrades to avoid being left in the dust by the first group.

Reconsider your short-term and intermediate decisions so you can afford the cost and effort needed for that upgrade.

C. You are part of a small or early-stage company, and know well how to use Outlook, ACT, Goldmine, and so forth to grow with current minimal resources. You've got your eye on the big time, when you'll get to worry about these issues in the prior two situations.

Whichever of the three situations you are in, pay attention to how best to access data as you grow larger and implement best sales practices where possible. These efforts will quickly pay for themselves.

Tip 7: Put in customer relationship management (CRM)

In contrast to Tip 6's sales force automation, Customer Relationship Management (CRM) systems aid in the management of a company's interactions with customers: potential and actual. These systems are wide-ranging, and lend themselves to automation.

Beyond aiding the sales process, CRM has marketing components, customer service elements, and customer technical support. Use CRM to attract potential clients, record and leverage their data, retain customers, win back the ones you've lost, and ensure retained customers stay happy. You'll find CRM aids in tracking marketing campaigns, helping you to evaluate your efforts.

Again, I recommend *CRM* magazine and its annual awards as a clearinghouse for you to weigh your CRM options. The magazine's 2011 winner in the enterprise, midmarket and small-business suite CRM was Salesforce.com, but you might consider Microsoft, Sugar CRM, and NetSuite. Each has vocal supporters.

Here are two very sound risk management reasons to trust your sales and marketing information to such systems:

A. *Know what you know.* For one thing, if a salesperson leaves, and your leads don't live in a centralized database—if they are just scribbled down on scraps of paper or in your salesperson's head—then your business will lose these leads. Pfft. Gone. This is wholly inefficient, and puts your sales and marketing operations at risk.

B. *Share what you know.* CRM encourages better tracking of sales and marketing, coordinating both for, say, customer interaction. Better communication and understanding of sales statuses between teams or individuals prevents two different salespeople from calling the same customer on the same day, a blunder that would likely fail to impress.

As a reminder, we discuss some risks with any solution, both legal and financial, way back in Chapter 1.

Tip 8: Harness search engine optimization (SEO)

Despite the widespread growth of the Internet and the fact that the buying public expects businesses to maintain a website, business leaders often do not know how to make their sites pop out in search results. This is where search engine optimization (SEO) comes in. It's something you need to invest in if you expect to stay competitive. SEO is a series of online marketing techniques that brings your website to the top of the first page (ideally) in search engines such as Google and Bing. How many times have you been willing to click to a second page of search results to find exactly what you were looking for? I'm going to guess that, unless you're conducting in-depth research, you're like most people and you click on hits that appear within inches of the top of your monitor, on the first page. That leaves a lot of marketers out in the cold. Don't join them there.

The rewards for smart SEO are clear: effective marketing, greater sales, and bigger payback. Although the "big guns" in your market (assuming you're not already the big guns) have likely hired an expert in this area, you can apply the same basic principles relating to keywords and keyword phrases that search engines look for when pulling pages for users.

Here's how it works:

Imagine you run a budget hostel in Dallas. Here's the sort of thing potential visitors are typing into their search engines:

- cheap hostel Dallas Texas
- budget hostel Dallas Texas
- cheap hotels Dallas
- cheap hostels Dallas
- Dallas cheap hostel
- budget accommodation in Dallas
- where to stay in Dallas, hostel

It's worth pointing out that while the fourth and fifth items may appear to be the same thing, they actually yield different search results. Look for good keywords for your business in Google AdWords. Then work these keywords and phrases into your website copy in such a way that they appear natural to the customer viewing your website.

There is a great deal more to search engine optimization than we have space for, but if your website is not optimized, get on it. This will create a better opportunity for you to achieve online and other sales, as customers have a better chance of finding out that your company exists and is an option for them.

Tip 9: Perform "seeding" or marketing trials

Once you have developed your product or service, and you've identified for whom it's most suitable, you may have an idea of how you are going to run your marketing campaign. A seeding trial helps you to determine if that approach would work before you roll it out on a wider scale. This is commonly carried out in software development as beta testing.

Seeding trials, in contrast, aim to reveal what elements of your product or service are most interesting to your customers. Use this push to build buzz and a support base for your product so that your initial "seed trial" customers help you to promote your product to their peers.

Did you receive a friend's invitation to join Google Plus, the social media platform launched in 2011? Did you extend an invitation to anyone among your contacts? An invitation is cachet. That's the idea in action.

In a seeding trial, you might give a product or service away at no cost to certain users as a means of building a groundswell of interest. Consider book or album reviews. You might send a free book or album link to key reviewers at blogs, newspapers, or magazines. It's free advertising for you if they like it, and you'll have something to tweet about. And again, this all feeds back into the sales funnel from our first tip.

Tip 10. Use the "long tail"

"Long tail" has gained in popularity as a model to describe the retailing strategy of selling a large number of unique items with relatively small quantities sold of each, usually in addition to selling fewer popular items in large quantities.

You don't always have to go all out to sell the most popular item or service. Instead, consider going after the long tail with your sales. The long tail method made even more popular by Amazon suggests that there are plenty of perfectly salable items in your inventory beyond the ones basking in the mainstream. Tap them for profit.

In this technique, you'll exploit niche markets for products or services. Amazon, for example, stocks familiar books with bestseller cachet, but also offers titles further from the bestseller lists that appeal to a substantial niche market in the aggregate. Amazon asks less for these titles. Because Amazon exploits Web technology, it's able to offer a vast inventory of niche titles that add up to big sales. The long tail sells a long range of products to niche markets.

Not every company can match Amazon's success with the long tail. Indeed, this is one reason traditional booksellers are starving—they only have so much shelf space. The lesson for some businesses that do not offer a lot of products is to identify niches and sell hard to those customers. Be distinctive. Break away from the pack. For appropriate situations, this will work well.

Of course, leveraging the long tail without considering all direct and indirect costs can cost more than you gain. This process often works best with a periodic overall review of product pricing and profitably for your entire product line.

Run the numbers to see how to apply this best.

Tip 11: Involve your sales and marketing teams in your decision-making
Sales and marketing are your business's front line. They meet with the customer or client, spend time getting to

QUESTIONS & ANSWERS

Jeffrey Milano |
CEO, The People's Chemist
Santa Fe, N.M.

ThePeoplesChemist.com is an online leader in natural medicine education and sales, direct through its own site, through Amazon, and in select retail outlets across America. The company describes its lab as a $1 million investment of love and passion for natural medicine, with all creations made in-house under FDA approved Good Manufacturing Practices (GMP), "with the absolute best science that modern day chemistry methods have to offer."

Gary Patterson: Jeffrey, how well would you say your leadership team is empowered to fight blind spots?

Jeffrey Milano: Anyone who is not responsible for his sphere of the organization is not going to be alert for blind spots, because they're not looking for them. And that starts with being given responsibility for the outcome of the business or the zone the team is working in. The leadership teams I've managed were given the responsibility to make their own decisions within their zone of operation, and I only stepped in when their decisions weren't nailing the desired result—and then, only to get them back on track.

If you want your team to be empowered to fight blind spots, whether financial sieves or production bottlenecks, give them responsibility for the products or the outcome. Otherwise, finding blind spots is your sole responsibility.

The individuals on each leadership team need to be trained to ensure they know what the product is; that they know exactly how to attain success; and that they have proven that they can perform without constant supervision. That makes turning over the responsibility easier.

Don't assume that someone who has a degree is trained and can get a product. Those people have an education, but they lack application, and application is everything. The world is full of armchair geniuses that don't know how to boil an egg. Training is an ongoing process, because as new people are trained, newer people will continue to be hired, and even others will retire or otherwise move on. Unless the organization is very small, training is a constant. People can always do things better, more efficiently, more effectively.

GP: How do you want to be told information that the deliverer might be reluctant to share?

JM: Getting my team to share information is an art, but it starts with an open door and a willingness to listen to anything people have to say without reacting to it. Easier said than done, but it's vital to keep the exchange of information going both ways.

GP: How have you encouraged your management team to share its core strengths and bedrock experiences so that everyone responsible for executing strategy is working from the same page?

JM: Within my current company, The People's Chemist as well as many others over the last 20 and more years, I've encouraged my management teams to write up their successful experiences (and unsuccessful ones) into training packs that we pass onto the next wave of those taking over. These packs become the "hats" we use to train others. Each hat includes the product of a particular position and all the actions that add up to how that product is attained. It includes advice from those who have had that hat previously—who may be part of senior management now.

In this way, we preserve and benefit from lessons learned so we don't repeat mistakes. It's costly enough for one person to make an expensive mistake, but if one person every two years makes the same costly mistake, then that's just stupid. Complete and thorough hats make strategy possible.

Otherwise, management spends all its time correcting mistakes and handling confusion that could have been avoided. Without hats and constant training, strategy is a constant battle. Imagine if the competition took this advice, but your own organization didn't. How well do you think you'd measure up?

Jeffrey Milano has a bachelor of science from Rider University, and decades of experience managing companies from small businesses to those in the Fortune 500. His expertise in organization and management helped propel The People's Chemist brand into a million-dollar-plus company without outside funding.

know customer or prospect needs, and really know conditions on the ground. Don't assume that you know best. Your sales and marketing team has a never-ending stream of tacit knowledge that you can leverage to support that relationship. Spend time with your teams to learn from them what your customers really want. They'll share successes and failures with you, and volunteer handy information that they have gleaned from your customers.

I've seen this work time and again.

- Marketing helped quantify a reasonable estimate of the value clients received from its service to help change product offerings and price at a technology company.
- Sales helped reorganize the manufacturing bill of materials logic to improve data accumulation for the estimating function to improve response time on common project revisions requested by prospects.
- Because several heads are likelier than one to come up with great ideas for customer interactions, the more time you spend brainstorming with your team the richer your rewards for your business. This can be as simple as bringing in lunch on Friday for informal updates and informational meetings.
- Another company took sales support, accounting and IT out to eat after hours for casual but fruitful discussions on improving operational and sales support processes.
- An offsite retreat of middle or top management to discuss strategic issues of sales and business model revisions can be highly effective when put together and facilitated correctly.

Tip 12: Apply the Pareto Principle

The Pareto Principle, also known as the 80/20 Rule, holds that you get 80 percent of your results from 20 percent of your efforts. What does that mean for sales and marketing? Look closely at your customers. Businesses typically find that 80 percent of their income comes from just 20 percent of their customer base. It's possible to focus on selling more to those customers.

Here's another way to look at this: for many businesses, 80 percent of your revenue or profit may come from just 20 percent of your products or services. Focus on really putting a lot more energy into selling the products or services that bring in the most net income. Then review the long tail (tip No. 5) in conjunction with a product profitability and pricing review to see where you can nab extra net profits.

Online companies, assess of the effectiveness of your Web pages in the same way. You may find that 80 percent of your online hits come from just 20 percent of your pages. In that case, focus on optimizing those stronger pages for a greater chance of closing the deal.

***

Your keen eye in tracking goals and objectives is essential. Focus on our top 12 secret tips for earning a greater payback from your sales and marketing efforts, and thrive:

Tip 1: Use the sales funnel

Tip 2: Measure sales team with "hit rate"

Tip 3: Sell solutions

Tip 4: Apply "guided selling"

Tip 5: Encourage upselling and cross selling

Tip 6: Implement sales work force management

Tip 7: Put in customer relationship management (CRM)

Tip 8: Harness search engine optimization (SEO)

Tip 9: Perform "seeding" or marketing trials

Tip 10: Use the "long tail"

Tip 11: Involve your sales and marketing teams in your decision-making

Tip 12: Apply the Pareto Principle

****

Functional areas could do a much better job communicating with their peers in other areas. These summaries pair one secret tip to a peer who needs to know more about sales. We follow that with five bedrock tips to use where you see the most value.

Secret Tips to Better Communicate With the:

Board – Tip 12: Apply the Pareto Principle

CEO – Tip 3: Sell solutions

CFO – Tip 1: Use the sales funnel

COO – Tip 2: Measure sales team with "hit rate"

CMO/CSO – Tip 7: Put in customer relationship management (CRM)

CTO/ CIO – Tip 8: Harness search engine optimization (SEO)

CPO/SVP-HR – Tip 6: Implement sales work force management

Frank Leadership Tips

Tip 4: Apply "guided selling"

Tip 5: Encourage upselling and cross selling

Tip 9: Perform "seeding" or marketing trials

Tip 10: Use the "long tail"

Tip 11: Involve your sales and marketing teams in your decision making

Whenever Sales speaks on such strategic issues, know that the boss (and boss's boss) is wondering:

I need to know!

I don't know

Why won't you tell me?

How can you tell me?

Help him fill in the blanks. Help your business sell more, provide higher customer value, attract and retain top talent, account for profits and losses and lead its industry.

Strategy on applying the issues you see through this process:

When you see a blind spot opportunity or risk, ask yourself all three of these concerns?

1. Do I have the courage to do something about this?
2. Do I have the passion to do it even though it is impossible to do?
3. Am I willing to share the glory to get this solved?

Coming up: How well do you understand your human relations and personnel department? Without meaning to, these dedicated workers may be hiding millions from you. To help uncover that money, let's get up close and personal with HR.

Chapter 6

Understanding Millions in Human Capital: What HR May Not Be Telling You

As we reveal hidden millions in human capital, let's focus on teamwork, for that's the name of the game.

Successful people build teams, and successful teams build industry-leading companies. That's a lesson for all of us, but especially for the entrepreneur who starts the business on the strength of a brilliant idea and a wallet full of credit cards. He might be reluctant to take on help or part with even a little control. But no one can—or should—go it alone every time. No matter your expertise, no matter your product or service, you're going to need help creating and accounting for value, setting and meeting goals, and scaling up for growth. You need people: human capital. You need a strong HR function and leader to help you build, lay claim, innovate, and calculate. Your leadership team is there to lead a loyal, well trained, and ambitious workforce, from managers to line workers to support staff. The tone you set at the top should resound, inspire, and spark value every day of every quarter.

Unfortunately, the human resources department slips in selling its core strengths and bedrock expertise within the enterprise. I've seen businesses sit on millions in untapped profit because HR keeps its light under a bushel. Most departments fail to grasp HR's full contribution and potential, and that keeps everyone in the dark.

Because it has developed the expertise to identify, hire, develop, and protect your company's chief asset, HR often feels it's enough that it meets its core tasks. Why, or how, would they take the time to convey its ins and outs to the wider management team?

Glad you asked.

HR staffers, read on to see what your CEO needs to know. Find out which of the following concepts you're inadvertently hiding from the team and thereby limiting your department's effectiveness. CEOs, read on to see what goes down in HR, and why you need to make that your business.

Let's bring in some key players: an accountant, a personal assistant, and an advisor/consultant. Here's why you need them, and how to get them:

The Accountant

With little exception, the wealthy and successful business people I've known kept a good accountant on the payroll, and had access to an external certified public accountant as well. At the very least, your accountant should work with you on year-end tax planning. I see too many rising executives who don't appreciate the value of a good accountant. I put that down to the fact that many people don't appreciate the value of measurement and relevant management information. More about this on deck for Chapter 7.

There is more to accountancy than just crunching numbers for business and financial needs. Your accountant can be your advisor and assistant across a broad range of professional and financial services. Indeed, the accountant is often a small business's most trusted adviser. They see things you might not.

The Personal Assistant

Call him a personal assistant or executive assistant, this aide has a battlefield role, one that is not easily scripted. It's a personal preference whether you hire on, and how much education your assistant should have, but be comfortable with the fit. The benefit to you is in having someone resourceful on hand to manage your finances, manage your calendar, plan your engagements, and coordinate routine administrative work so that you can concentrate on your business.

Delegating is hard for a lot of us, particularly when we're starting out or are uncertain about next steps. But you must get comfortable with this skill. You're on the job to weigh the risks and chart the course.

The Adviser/Consultant

In business, the owner-manager will face occasions that call for a consultant: someone who deals with areas outside the accountant's realm. The need may feel vague, or the owner-manager might suspect the solution is beyond his or her inclination or background. For example, an auto body shop owner may be interested in new market penetration. A marketing consultant can help.

It is also true that time, finances, and staff resources are limited, so it's important to justify bringing in a consultant. There's a broad range of issues that are suitable for consulting projects: those which are **internal**, such as establishing systems and procedures as the business takes a transition to a turnkey approach; or those that are **external**, such as investigating market potential for a new product.

Consultants offer perspective and talent on subjects from sales to financial management and from human resources to training. Consultants are typically brought in for their expertise and fresh view.

Working with a consultant is an opportunity to do creative problem solving, and should, by definition, be rewarding. Pass on the ones who tell you at the outset what they're going to do to help you; their methodology might not apply to your case. Trust those who take the time to get to know your situation and goals.

Common consultant functions for growth businesses:

- *Customer-sales enhancement.* There is a wealth of work being done in the customer relationship management (CRM) arena, from the simple area of technology improvement—using call centers and the like—to techniques for developing a more systematic, across-the-business approach to handling and growing your customer base.

- *Strategic financial management.* You'll benefit from periodic reviews of financial reports and business procedures for maintaining good financial measurement, forecasting, and tracking. Such consultants evaluate profitability, cash flow, and collections; identify strengths and weaknesses such as poor management of the receivables; and help business owners hit financial management benchmarks.

- *Training and team building.* Many consultancies are known for training and team-building. Commonly, small businesses seeking a sales boost tap *ad hoc* consultants to build synergy and supercharge team efforts. They give leaders valuable insights into the dynamics that affect team processes and recommend improvements.

The Case for Hiring

What about the next steps? Should you look beyond consultants and freelancers and hire an employee? Take advantage of this checklist, and decide for yourself:

- List the various tasks you expect your new employee to perform. Write a detailed job description. Be specific and estimate the time required to do the work. This will help you decide whether you need to add a full-time employee, a part-time employee, or more than one employee.
- You will need to compete in the marketplace on pay and benefits, so do your homework. The U.S. Bureau of Labor Statistics is a great resource on this issue. Include salary, benefits, and taxes. Consider how much you'll pay (in money and time) in training. Even when you hire a sharp, solid candidate, he will need to learn your preferred methods, solutions, and routines.
- How much will it cost to advertise, screen applicants, interview them, and so forth? Will the employee add revenues and/or enhance efficiencies? Ideally, your new staffer will free you from routine work so you can develop business opportunities. If so, will the profits of the company increase by more than what you expect to pay the new hire? If not, you may not be ready to hire.
- Hire for attitude; train for skills. An employee may be highly skilled, but that means nothing if he lacks passion and team focus.

When to Promote

A common pitfall: Small businesses entering a rapid growth phase tend to promote employees beyond their ability, rather than recruit new staff with the necessary skills. It's easy to see why: the company lacks HR expertise and planning. Some small enterprises may have formal plans detailing how they will grow their business; few boast a manpower plan outlining how they will resource that growth.

At this point, such business operators are better off bringing in outside talent (a marketing manager for example) instead of promoting a generalist for some crucial spots where near-term crucial expertise is not available. Then HR can help transition from external to internal staffing with an emphasis on succession planning, and create a career path for talented employees and set standards for ambitious staff in achieving promotion.

Workers do leave jobs, particularly when they're motivated but don't see a way to advance. When a business loses such staff, it also loses significant business knowledge—sales contacts and relationships, for example (see Chapters 4 and 5 on sales). You've got to help such workers succeed with you. Failing that, you've got to properly document their lack of expertise.

Again, a current job description increases your chances of attracting the right person; a sketchier job description nets a number of similar applicants perhaps less suited to the job and makes for a more subjective selection process. Without job descriptions, organizations can hardly set reasonable performance indicators or carry out performance reviews—essential tools that help businesses and employees identify, structure, track, and document performance goals.

Thought leader Jim Collins discusses in *Good to Great* the importance of getting the right people "on the bus." Collins argues that if the wrong people board the bus in the first place, then the organization won't succeed—it'll simply peter along, never achieving greatness. Getting the right people in the right seats on the bus is an essential human capital skill; doing it right helps earn the HR head a seat at the table.

Motivating and Retaining Employees

An increasingly mobile workforce and surging demand for talent constitute a real challenge to retaining valuable employees. You will do well to reward your people with fair pay and benefits, but you must also recognize that people need a purpose beyond remuneration to keep them enthusiastic, engaged, and loyal.

Here's how:

- *Offer meaningful work.* If you find ways to help people enjoy their daily work, you'll boost their job performance. If you treat your employees respectfully, and prove you value their input, they'll do well for themselves and the company.

- *Just ask.* Employers who don't try to understand workers' career objectives run the risk of de-motivating their workforce—and will find themselves endlessly seeking replacements for key people. Ask what their expectations are and try to meet them. Even small things can make people happy—it doesn't require budget-breaking initiatives to satisfy staff needs.

- Despite the best intentions, many employers aren't very good at asking employees what they need, meeting those needs, and keeping them from jumping ship. Do you recognize your employees' needs?

What Employees Want

Fairly universal needs include job security, interesting work, and the promise of career advancement for competent contributors. Tools for self-assessment and in-house learning as well as development opportunities and succession planning are crucial for organizations to create adequate career-advancement strategies for employees. A business adopting these fundamental policies is likely to retain key employees.

Too many companies skate over thin ice by relying exclusively on a passive technique such as performance reviews, or else nothing at all. If those companies had any talent, they might look to move up where they would be appreciated and rewarded. Keep your eyes peeled for these people.

Treat your people well, and they'll treat each other—and you—very well. Compare your efforts toward establishing achievement, loyalty, and respect against this checklist. How well do you implement the following tactics?

- *Ensure job descriptions are very clear* and thus let your employees know exactly what you expect from them. Make it clear what it would take for an employee to be assured of advancement within the business. Build this assurance into the job description.

- *Give employees motivating and meaningful work,* and empower them to make decisions within their jobs necessary to obtain the results you seek. Most successful business people will tell you how hard it is, at least initially, to get accustomed to delegating. But it pays off in time, money, energy, morale, and accountability.

- *Provide opportunities for employees to learn new skills.* Offer internal and external training. If possible, have staff participate in industry events in other cities or countries to gain a richer perspective on your customers and vendors, and strengthen your contacts across the globe.

- *Provide performance-review feedback* to your employees at least every six months. Make a point of recognizing employees for good work.

- If possible, *allow workers flexibility in their schedules* with flextime, part-time, and telecommuting opportunities. Today's workers, particularly younger ones, are accustomed to a strong sense of autonomy. Let them propose how they'll best get the job done, and support them in any way you can as long as it helps the business.

succeed in business you need to conduct team meetings that give most or all of the staff the benefit of your vision, allow for an open exchange of ideas, build support for initiatives, report on progress, and air grievances.

Consistency is key. When people know they'll be called on to contribute, they tend to organize their thoughts, pull in facts, and generally pay closer attention to what's going on around them. You can plan a monthly meeting for the entire company, and perhaps weekly get-togethers for various action teams. Such meetings should reflect the goals established for your business units.

In addition to fostering the transfer of information, meetings also help motivate staff and nurture good corporate sprit and culture (more on culture in a bit). They are an excellent way to build team skills, both in terms of leadership and organization.

HR is ideally suited to encourage more of the strategic conversations mentioned in the introduction. Who needs to know what you know? How can we help you pass that information along?

Sometimes the most effective ways of motivating employees are also the easiest. People usually want to do a good job and they want to be recognized for it. Recognition can come in many forms, some of which cost little. You can hardly offer a more powerful recognition for a job well done than offering that person a more challenging or higher-profile project.

Financial Incentives for Employees

Money talks. Paying people more than they expect is a great way to attract loyalty, feed innovation, and sustain motivation. It's recognition that endorses his or her value to the business. If the entire team were motivated by the extra dollars, then you'd have a powerful driver for business performance. The

QUESTIONS & ANSWERS

Margaret J. King, PhD |
Director, Center for Cultural Studies & Analysis
Philadelphia, Pa.

Margaret J. King, PhD, is director of the Center for Cultural Studies & Analysis, a think tank which decodes how consumers determine value in products, concepts, and ideas. Corporations, themed environments, museums, and educational venues apply her organization's gathered intelligence in human factors to new product development, marketing and advertising, and strategic planning.

Gary Patterson: Dr. King, how might we start thinking of our workforce if we want to engage them and challenge them to help take responsibility for the big picture?

Margaret J. King: This is what "people as assets" really means. This is the entrepreneurial view of employment: as leasing the creative thinking and innovative power of experts. We are far beyond thinking about employees as maintenance workers. These human assets are now expected to be proactive promoters of the company's real equity and interests. This model is the work-culture basis of the information age.

GP: We often encourage leadership and management to "think outside the box." It sounds like a cliché to many. But what are the advantages?

MK: Promoting and rewarding leadership and entrepreneurship versus paying for managing and carrying out instructions is what sponsoring ingenuity means. Initiative and risk-taking have to be rewarded as it involves operating above your job description. This requires a new sophistication on the part of business to trust this process. It also, of course, requires a fresh and heightened outlook on recruitment, hiring, and retention.

In my view, HR is several decades behind the curve in still looking in résumés for loyalty, obedience, and dronish work habits. These are easier to judge than new cultural values. We need a new kind of perception for a flatter work structure built on professional values versus traditional industrial expectations.

GP: We are arguing for rewards that inspire productivity, but we don't want to give away the store. How much is just enough?

MK: The entire reward system is what drives decision-making and behavior. It's imperative to look objectively at the rewards that drive your business in fact rather than in theory. Change the rewards, and changes in behavior will quickly follow. For information-age employment, money isn't the chief driver, though it still resides at the very bottom line. Prestige, colleagueship, opportunity for growth and learning, flextime, and other social and cognitive awards are actually more motivational. Subway's current campaign stars high-achieving alumni to recruit this type of aspirational workforce. And it doesn't involve giving away anything at all; it just involves identifying what people put the highest value on besides money, then finding ways to deliver.

GP: How should executives think about culture for best effect?

MK: What are the themes within the culture? How do people get hired, fired, promoted, rewarded? These are the real "tells" of any cultural system. And most organizations are quite unaware of how these operate—and by what value system—until things start to fall apart, when it's far too late for remedial action. That's why cultural analysis can unravel from the outside the basic value dynamics behind the business. The best understand at some level how they need to operate (and how not), based largely on the people dynamic.

GP: We say culture is really just the sum of our people's attitudes, and those attitudes stem from leaders' vision, passion, fairness, and commitment. Is that a fair description of culture?

MK: Yes, when it's an ethical one. That's the ideal, because people are social primates, and as such, live in social systems: families, communities, business, nations. We need most of all to understand our own values for preferred states: what we call ideals. Some of these are group-specific, while others are universal.

Margaret J. King is a nationally recognized expert on theme parks and consumer behavior. She received the first graduate degree ever awarded in popular culture from the Center for the Study of Popular Culture, and the Ph.D. in American Studies from the University of Hawaii. Research at the Culture Learning Institute at the East-West Center included fieldwork in Tokyo and Kyoto. Most of her work involves explaining the workings of American cultural values to American business.

Formal and Informal Appreciation Devices

Honest communication allows workers to improve their performance, seek clarification on expectations; and it empowers everyone to participate in your company's business planning. How you communicate can be **formal** or **informal**. To question, of course, is how much? Complete market studies to determine where you want to be relative to completion and local markets.

If you're banking extra sales and working smarter, you'll see a plumper bottom line; you can and should invest in appropriate wage and salary increases. Look at profit-linked incentive performance as a way of investing in future productivity. You're free to allocate a greater percentage of the budget against such costs on the basis that it results in an overall improvement in margins and absolute profits.

Profit Sharing

Profit sharing or bonus programs are employee incentives in which the business sets aside a portion of the company's profits at year-end for distribution to the employees. When such systems are adopted, it is amazing to see how employees become abundantly interested in the amount of money spent on tea and cookies! They become absolute fiends about wasteful overheads. One contact recently told me that the very day his company announced its share of net income program, a delegation of staff presented more than 50 examples of waste and inefficiencies they'd uncovered in the business!

Think profit sharing through. If you're going that route, set clear linkages between performance and profit sharing reward. Profit sharing can hurt the business if it fails to reward the deserving and if it sparks resentment among non-recipients. Integrate this program into your business's other benefit programs for an overall attractive total benefits package that rewards top performers. Set the stage for profit sharing. Overemphasizing short-term profits detracts from long-term profitability. Balance these needs with corporate culture.

You or your accountant should know your threshold for acceptable profitability. This could be an absolute minimum target, a percentage of total revenues, or it could relate to some return on the owner's equity in the business. This is your basis for an effective profit sharing program.

Be sure to consider:

- *Profit threshold.* Establish a profit target before profit sharing kicks in.
- *Percentage of profits*: set and discuss the percentage of profits your employees may be qualified to share. Do this in advance of cutting the checks. Make the math well known beforehand as an incentive and a warning. For example, you may say that you're setting aside 10 percent of all profits over $100,000 for the employee profit sharing program.
- *Who participates?* You get to decide. Will it be only those who directly affect bottom-line results, such as salespeople? Will they be the only participating members? You might decide that, although the amount in the profit sharing pool is fixed, management may select recipients based on some fair criteria.
- *How to share.* Once you know with whom, settle on how. You might set profit share distribution equal across the board, or tailor them to each employee's remuneration level, where the distribution gets divided according to each person's respective share of the overall payroll. Some businesses require at least six months' continuous employment before the employee is qualified to share.

Mixed and Unusual Perks

Employers are remarkably imaginative when it comes to employee perks (from "perquisite," a thing regarded as a special right or privilege enjoyed as a result of one's position). A company car or car allowances are nice when possible, but people also appreciate help with special parenting needs such as payment of private health insurance, pet care, and so on.

As a business owner, of course, you know that all these perks are a business cost, so justify them in terms of morale and retention value. And perks need to fit the culture. Consider pets in the workplace. Some industries welcome dogs at the desk as friendly companions; others don't want Rover anywhere near their hard-working employees.

Not every perk will interest every employee. But here are some other ideas that might boost performance and even involve your business more with your local business community, which is common sense and a good PR move:

- *Massages.* This is popular in both small and large enterprises: workers get neck and back massages at their desks. Good for ergonomic health, a nice break, and it's fun.
- *Day-care facilities.* Many companies provide on-site child-care facilities to take the pressure off two-income families or single parents.
- *Health club membership.* Fit employees are healthy, alert, and productive. You might strike a deal with the gym for discounts on referrals or some other cross promotion;
- *Office meal delivery.* Have meals delivered from off-site as an extension of the required meal allowance. We think of pizza as the go-to treat, but there are healthier options for working out of normal office or factory hours late into the night.

Such perks enhance productivity and morale, and immediately improve the employee's life in some way that they'll remember and associate with you. Employees who are less distracted by lack of childcare, limited opportunities to eat and socialize with co-workers, and aches and pains at the desk or factory floor will focus more on the job at hand.

Remember, the key to long-term business success is involving employees in your vision and then letting them run with it. Tap employees' ingenuity and creativity to enhance existing benefits. After all, you don't want to have to come up with all the ideas yourself. Include your people and you'll go farther.

The Payoff: A Winning Culture

How does all this talk of perks sit with you? Does it seem excessive? In my experience, sponsoring ingenuity among employees is smart, productive, and required. After all, business is about employing people for fair, market-related remuneration to help create buyer value, and profits for business owners: the visionaries and risk-takers.

We've come a long way from the sweatshops of the 19th century. It's no accident that buzzwords such as "corporate culture" and "work-life balance" prevail even in a brutal economy. Contemporary best-business practices demand an enlightened approach.

We've talked about corporate culture. What is it? Culture is simply a way of doing things, and it's inevitable. You don't get to decide whether to have a corporate culture, but you can decide whether yours will be healthy and will help create value. Creating a healthy culture creates a context for everything that people do. It gives work meaning. It gives employees direction. It implements your vision. In the end, it boosts profits.

The problem with many companies is that they don't understand culture—theirs or their competitors'. In my experience, if you challenge most chief executives to define corporate culture or describe theirs, they wouldn't understand the

We're All in this Together, or We Should Be

Always let your right hand know what your left hand is doing.

I recall a poorly capitalized $40 million holding company whose people stretched to operate a strategic five-year initiative to profitably grow to $100 million. A noble, exciting challenge. Unfortunately, these folks soon learned they bore a $5 million albatross on their backs: economic losses for deferred maintenance and underperforming assets in non-core markets.

Here was a profound disconnect between management and the board of directors. The company was running without common incentives and goals between management and the board, and they were diluting their efforts at huge cost.

The cure? Communication. We brought management and the board together, and soon they were rowing in the same direction.

What were management and the board missing? We compiled, in a readable, actionable format, the magnitude and timing of the $5 million non-financial statement impairment. We set aside the lofty five-year, $100 million strategic growth initiative, and plotted our plan to knock out that albatross. A complete success.

Are you and your teammates reading the same playbook?

---

question. "What do you mean? We're the second largest manufacturer of piston grommets on the East Coast."

Your culture is really just the sum of your people's attitudes. And those attitudes stem from leaders' vision, passion, fairness, and commitment.

So, how do you shape culture?

- First, you recognize that great employers *nurture a culture* consistent with their business vision and goals. Each year, *Fortune* publishes an annual listing of the top

100 companies to work for with discussion on selection criteria. How do you compare?

- Businesses with great cultures set *clear goals and values* and live by them. Compare your efforts here. Why do people join your team? Why do they leave? What else are they looking for that might passionately connect them to your business's strategy and goals?

- Although businesses usually set goals, they are prone to tuck them away in a binder in a back office. A small business might mount its mission statement at the front door and employees might pay it lip service, but that doesn't add up to buy-in. Your people need to *feel a sense of ownership of the business mission*. When staff understands what the business is about, their morale and motivation rise high. This is your job: live your mission. Set the tone. Call out staffers you see doing it right.

- Just as important in cultivating a great corporate culture is a *great communications flow*. It's the hallmark of all great business leaders, from the small two- or three-person business right through to the global giants. Help employees connect to the decision-making process, as it encourages ownership of the results. Good communication doesn't require a weekly meeting, just a consistently scheduled forum where management report on the state of the business in specific terms to do with those items that matter: profit and milestones to encourage personal or team ownership.

- *Teamwork* (with which we started this Chapter) is a major factor in developing superior corporate cultures. Successful teams build successful enterprises, and these become known as great places to work and do business with. Employees enjoy their work when they are part of a winning culture. They take pride in themselves, their product, their contribution to society, and you.

Implementing even a few of these ideas will go a long way toward building a small business that will be a great place to work—and all things being equal, will prosper. Be patient: it may take up to two years to see the results of the effort. Better still: build it in at the outset, if you have that chance.

*　*　*

BEDROCK CONCEPTS RECAP

Successful people build teams and successful teams build industry-leading companies.

Accountants provide valuable measurement and relevant management information.

Personal or executive assistants can be exceptional employees, adding value to your business life while saving you time, money, and energy.

Consultants can address key internal or external concerns, bringing expertise you don't have.

Hire for attitude; train for skills.

If you treat your employees with respect and prove that you value their input, they'll be motivated to do well for themselves and for the company.

Treat your people well, and they'll treat each other—and you—very well.

Honest communication allows workers to improve their performance and seek clarification on expectations—and empowers everyone to participate in your company's business planning.

Let your workers share the profits. They helped create it, and you'll earn their buy-in.

Perks enhance productivity and morale, and immediately improve the employee's life in some way they'll remember and associate with you.

A successful culture that nurtures personal growth and development is one that supports good business. You get to set the tone.

Coming up: to accelerate momentum in that business and exploit those missing millions in human resources, Chapter 7 provides 12 secret tips: focused tactics to help you tap the full benefits of a supercharged HR throughout the business.

Chapter 7

Uncover Millions in Human Capital

In Chapter 6, the whole team discovered human resources' bedrock concepts. Now we can put that knowledge to work in chasing down your hidden millions.

Human relations people, leverage this chapter to give your peers insight into propelling business profitability from your point of view. Everyone else: learn here how to support HR, and really tap the potential of new hires, established teams, and former loose cannons. You can grow the bottom line by millions in supporting HR.

Here's how:

Sales and marketing are moving products and services to cost effectively follow their charter. Operations is ready to deliver the goods efficiently, meeting customer expectations without giving away the store. Make sure you've got the right people for the job and are treating them well. Without the right people, you are dramatically underperforming your potential and limiting your people. Some would say that you don't have a business. The good news is that you don't necessarily need buckets of cash to motivate your staff. Some people are highly motivated by money, but research shows most people are motivated by a broad variety of other factors. Are you addressing them all?

You'll find your path neatly laid out for you in "One More Time: How Do You Motivate Employees?" a classic paper published in the *Harvard Business Review*. In it, psychologist

Frederick Herzberg proposes the Motivation-Hygiene Theory, also known as the Two-factor theory (1959) of job satisfaction. According to Herzberg, two sets of factors influence job satisfaction: motivation and hygiene.

Motivation factors:

- Achievement
- Recognition
- The work itself
- Responsibility
- Promotion
- Growth

Hygiene factors (which are cyclical in nature, and loop back to a starting point, as in "What have you done for me lately?"):

- Pay and benefits
- Company policy and administration
- Relationships with co-workers
- Supervision
- Status
- Job security
- Working conditions
- Personal life

This is worth your time. Herzberg's paper is a bestseller, and you'll learn a lot from its supporters and critics. Here's an excerpt, in which Herzberg describes his hypothesis and shows how it applies to management. By way of background, Herzberg collected his data from interviews with a statistically significant population of accountants and engineers in the Pittsburgh area:

> Briefly, we asked our respondents to describe periods in their lives when they were exceedingly happy and unhappy

with their jobs. Each respondent gave as many "sequences of events" as he could that met certain criteria—including a marked change in feeling, a beginning and an end, and contained some substantive description other than feelings and interpretations...

The proposed hypothesis appears verified. The factors on the right that led to satisfaction (achievement, intrinsic interest in the work, responsibility, and advancement) are mostly unipolar; that is, they contribute very little to job dissatisfaction. Conversely, the dis-satisfiers (company policy and administrative practices, supervision, interpersonal relationships, working conditions, and salary) contribute very little to job satisfaction. [Herzberg, "The Motivation-Hygiene Concept and Problems of Manpower" *Personnel Administration* (January–February 1964). 3–7]

If you harness that knowledge, your people will thank you for it. Two-factor theory shows how pay and benefits, a hygiene factor, can demotivate employees; they should not be a focus for cash-strapped organizations. Yes, offer attractive pay and benefits, but avoid waving a fistful of dollars at your employees. It won't boost performance on its own. Instead, review motivation and hygiene factors to focus on what you *can* offer rather than what you can't. Promotions usually cost money because they involve a new job title and wider responsibilities. But other factors cost nothing and produce results. Take your pick: achievement, recognition, the work itself, responsibility, and growth.

In light of what Herzberg says, and in the interest of expanding your motivation toolkit, here are 12 secret tips for improving your return on effort on HR.

Tip 1: Get the right person for the job

Who are the right people? According to Jim Collins, leading organizations work hard to fit the right people to the right tasks. Fiscal success relates directly to hiring the right people and keeping them on board. It also requires recognizing when a person ought not to stay in the organization, and managing his exit from the task as soon as possible. Overall, it costs less to dump a consistently poor performer than to keep him. Businesses lose money by hanging on to people should step off the bus at the next stop. See Tips 10 and 11 for additional thoughts on this point.

Effective businesses hire talent who provide good value for the money and who add value to the business. I don't mean the cheapest guys you can get for your dollar, but the ones who have a lot to offer, and who strive to be the best--your top performers. Invest in the right people for your business. It sounds obvious, but there's a special skill and separate procedures involved. The key human resources interfaces in this instance are the **hiring process** and the **performance management system.**

Because there's so much at stake, spend the time to work out a thorough job description, as described in Chapter 6. Respect your intuition, too. If your gut tells you that a candidate, even one who looks great on paper, came highly recommended, and interviewed well enough is a poor fit, then odds are that person is wrong for your team. Think about having more people involved in the interviewing process and share candid results.

Tip 2: Implement coaching in your organization

With the right people in place, train them using coaching and mentoring. In the absence of a big budget for training and development, and with on-the-job training gathering steam, consider ramping up your coaching efforts. Coaches guide people to perform at their best.

Have you ever wondered about the origins of the word "coach"? It refers to "carriage," a medium of transport, helping someone get from where he is to where he wants to be.

In business, the practice is an establishing discipline. A 2004 Association for Coaching study shows that the numbers support it. The study found:

- 48 percent of coaching "purchasers" agreed that having a quantifiable measure on return on investment from coaching is important;
- 38 percent of the same respondents reported that coaching re-engages individuals, and leads to increased productivity;
- 53 percent reported coaching increased job motivation; and
- 58 percent reported gains in people management skills. Coaching provides personal development that aids leadership, team building, sales, and negotiation. An effective coach gives practical, supportive feedback, and helps the recipient learn to choose the wisest course of action for a given situation.

As a takeaway, here's more detail on coaching via the Kolb Learning Cycle, the underpinnings of this essential business practice. We see how coaching aids in reflection about experiences—and leads to more effective ways of working:

The Kolb Learning Cycle

Wherever you start in the cycle, think of this as a circular flow, which includes four elements, as my diagram below shows:

1. **Experience.** Doing something action-oriented leads to…
2. **Experimenting.** Testing out conclusions leads to…
3. **Reflecting.** Observing what actually happened leads to…
4. **Conceptualizing.** Coming to conclusions, which are useful for next time, leads to…

Coaching works. In contrast with costly training courses, coaching offers distinct and important advantages, particularly in meeting the unique needs of the person being coached. In a training class with many participants, that's probably not going to happen. Coaching takes time, which is a cost; but when cash is scarce, it's an investment in your people that you can easily make and won't regret.

Tip 3: Create mentor and buddy systems

Build on coaching with mentoring and buddy systems to offer development benefits for participants and power motivation at small expense.

Similar to coaching, a **mentor** is a person who guides another through his/her career. Where coaches are often the coachee's direct line manager, mentors are experienced or senior individuals working in the same department, business, industry, or a similar field in a different industry. The ideal mentor is someone the mentee respects and admires. As with coaching, the relationship targets specific learning needs.

A **buddy system** is a little different. Buddy employees usually share a level in the organization, and help each other solve problems, gain perspective, skills, and other resources. Mentoring and buddy systems help motivate in that they demonstrate to the employee the company's commitment to his or her personal and professional development.

Tip 4: Empower your team

Empowerment is an excellent motivator. It imbues the employee with responsibility, which leads to personal growth. Invest your time productively by reviewing job descriptions, looking at upcoming projects, and reviewing which staff will be motivated by which tasks. Analysis spent in this area may reap huge rewards in terms of both motivation and productivity. You can sell such activities to employees as résumé-boosting benefits and paths to advancement.

A note on pitching projects to employees: while it is motivating to earn more responsibility and achieve new goals, remember that pay and benefits is a hygiene factor. If the employee thinks that he is being asked to perform tasks way above what was agreed contractually, then the pay and benefits issue will rear its head. Respect the boundaries you agreed to when you made the hire, or negotiate new ones.

Tip 5: Make the work exciting

If the work itself seems enjoyable and interesting, and offers opportunities for growth, employees will pin less importance on pay and benefits. Find out what makes your employees tick, and encourage them. Create excitement about what's going on. Innovation is exciting, and people take pride in working on new ideas, in new markets, in new directions, with new tools. Make sure that when you talk with your people you reveal your own enthusiasm, which is bound to rub off on the team, and foster buy-in. Ever given a pep talk? Are you comfortable with public speaking? If not, consider membership in Toastmasters International, the public speaking and leadership development club where you can learn to persuade, inform, entertain, inspire, and motivate a variety of audiences.

Courage, Conviction, and Results

Failure can lead to some of the greatest success you've ever known if you take the time and care to learn from it.

Gary moved from operations into sales for a commercial debt management firm as a major career change. The economy was not good. He learned he was assigned the worst performing district in the country—and that his three predecessors had failed. That's tough. That's a challenge.

What were we missing? As we dug into this, we saw the scope of the issues before us in needing a stronger sales pipeline, and a mechanism to close more of the leads the pipeline produced.

I recommended several solutions, and the one we implemented was leveraging cutting-edge technology to cull an inexpensive source of timely leads for the sales funnel, increasing its size and quality. Then we worked with customers to encourage them to create strategies for moving forward to success while we used our expertise to settle those past debts and obligations and commitments, rather than let the past destroy the future.

All in a day's work. The district sailed from worst to best within a year. Gary did well and was rewarded for the value he helped create, and which added to his skills. That Gary is me.

What challenges are you willing to tackle even though they seem impossible? You might be surprised at what you can accomplish.

Tip 6: Think through pay raises and training

Research shows that small merit-pay increases may do more harm than good. Consider throwing out the average raises and give those who are contributing a decent merit raise and those who aren't nothing. Then do what you should have done in the first place. Manage out of the organization, those who aren't performing out of the organization. More on this approach in Tips 10 and 11.

Another warning: when finances are scarce, you may be tempted to cut back on training and development. Proceed carefully. Training and development are important motivators, and are proven champs at bolstering productivity and the bottom line.

Forget surveys and consider how often most companies, yours included, say that people are the organization's most important asset.

The common sense answer supports a range of studies which analyzed the financial performance of companies that invest in training and development as compared against to those that don't. The companies that invested in employees earned higher sales per employee.

Don't be fooled by any blips in apparent ROI when slashing training budgets during hard times. These are valuable programs and you'll lose out in the end by snubbing them. The challenge is to make this case to leadership, which may want to put it on the chopping block as difficult to quantify and generally just too great a risk.

On-the-job training (OJT) reaps the rewards of training and development even when those programs are threatened. It should be an easy sell, as it doesn't rely on a glossy $3,000 leadership development or team-building course. OJT usually makes an appearance at the employee's induction before it is eventually dropped. Pick it up and dust it off to give your employees a richer involvement in the organization's mission, build their skill sets, and help them participate in the kind of strategic conversations that could save you millions.

Tip 7: Find cost-effective and innovative ways to meet employee needs

One enterprising organization I worked with kept employees on the same page for training and development by launching

QUESTIONS & ANSWERS

Roberta Matuson |
President, Human Resource Solutions
Northampton, Mass.

For more than 25 years, Roberta Matuson, president of Human Resource Solutions, has helped leaders in Fortune 500 companies including Best Buy, New Balance, The Boston Beer Company and small to medium-size businesses, create exceptional workplaces leading to extraordinary results. She is a leading authority on leadership and the skills and strategies required to earn employee commitment and client loyalty.

GARY PATTERSON: Roberta, what's your perspective on merit raises?

ROBERTA MATUSON: I say throw out the average raises, and give those who are contributing a decent merit increase and those who aren't, nothing. Then do what you should have done in the first place: manage those who aren't performing out of the organization.

GP: What should companies be focusing on, from your perspective, to save the most time and money?

RM: In my experience, the most important piece is hiring for fit. Do this well and you won't have to worry about many of the headaches that usually occur with bad hires.

GP: That said, how can companies get a handle on turnover costs?

RM: While companies know replacing an employee costs considerable time, energy, and lost productivity, few can put a dollar figure on the actual cost. Lack of hard data means investments in retention and recruitment programs get placed on the back burner.

The cost of turnover estimates for a single position range from thirty percent of the yearly salary for hourly employees to 150 percent, as estimated by the Saratoga Institute. The McQuaig Institute puts this into terms that most of us can relate to. A fast food restaurant must sell 7,613 children's combo meals at $2.50 each to recoup the cost of losing just one crewmember. To recoup the cost of losing just one sales clerk, a clothing store must sell almost 3,000 pairs of khakis at $35. How many of your products or services must you sell to make up for one employee?

These examples represent the cost of turnover, which encompasses replacement costs, training costs, separation costs, and lost productivity. You may be thinking that positions in your company are considerably more sophisticated than those found in fast food restaurants or retail organizations, and that it's impossible to come up with a number. But even an approximate number is better than no number at all.

Calculating your cost of turnover is simpler than you think. Begin by looking at everyone who has left your organization this year. If you want to capture a full year's worth of information, consider capturing the data for those who left the company the previous year as well. The business costs and impact of employee turnover can be grouped into four major categories: 1) costs due to a person leaving, 2) hiring costs, 3) training costs, and 4) lost productivity costs. [Covered in depth at www.yourhrexperts.com].

Once an employee has announced his resignation, he has begun to transition out of the company. While working out his notice period, his full attention is no longer on your business. Others in the organization are picking up his slack, which prohibits them from giving full attention to their own jobs.

Closely examine the costs associated with each person leaving, then plug this information into a spreadsheet to determine the real cost of employee turnover in your organization. How do you measure up? Are you in better shape than you thought or is it time for an intervention?

Given the high costs involved and the impact on productivity and customer retention, a well thought-out retention program can easily pay for itself over and over again.

Employee turnover is a lot like eating dark chocolate. In moderation, both are fine and can even be healthy. In excess, both can have serious ramifications.

an enjoyable book club. Supplying the books and the time to discuss them costs significantly less than sending the same staff out to a dry, remote course to be lectured over the same material. Staff found the reading and discussion fun, productive, and fostered team-building. Everybody wins.

Tip 8: Manage expectations

Say you don't have much money on hand for bonuses or large pay rises. Should you keep that from the team? No. Be relatively open about this, or at the very least, refrain from promising something you can't deliver. There's nothing more effective at demotivating staff than looking forward to a promised reward and then not getting it. If there isn't much money to spare, know that money is simply one of several motivators, and focus on what you *can* do for your employees. For example, if pay raises are out, you can certainly afford to cut a hard-working team member a spontaneous three-day weekend. Never make promises you can't keep—set the tone and a healthy culture—and your employees won't either.

Tip 9: Balance "thank you" and tough love

Thank your employees and recognize them when they do a great job. Often, employers are quick to point out an employee's failings and overlook their accomplishments. A thank-you is free and it highlights superb performance. In addition to it being common courtesy, it's good business sense. Buy these folks a thoughtful but modest gift—say, a bottle of wine—for exceptional effort (even effort that was followed by a poor outcome, if it was a learning experience).

Of course, a handwritten thank you note from one's superior often ranks sweeter than a bottle of wine. The note costs less, may be savored longer, and the employee can use it to prove his value when he seeks to advance.

You should also to review your organization regularly from a fresh perspective. Employees correctly value and appreciate the attention, and it gives you both actionable information. Use tough love where necessary. Were you to reboot your business, which positions and skill sets would you need on hand? How does that compare to what you've got? Make the change.

Tap a concept often used on projects, strategic analyses or business in general to create HR's version of a Gap or SWOT analysis, which can highlight existing and projected strengths and weaknesses, and reveal a range of alternatives.

Businesses use SWOT to find areas to improve--that is, blind spots.

- Which skills do your employees not fully exploit in their current position?

- Where can you incorporate training, development, or coaching programs to help current staff?
- When and how should you train, develop, or coach someone to move to another position, thereby rewarding employee loyalty and organizational knowledge?

What happens when you can't turn an employee's weakness into strength? Having identified the need for change, ask yourself:

- When and how should you demote an employee?
- Who no longer fits in the organization and should be let go?

Effective performance management saves the company money over the long haul in reduced business risk and fewer flat-out mistakes.

Leaders must understand and avoid the sunk-cost fallacy, which all too often sucks decision makers down a hole. We sometimes feel that we've got so much invested in this option; it would be foolish to bail out now. Know when it's time to bail. Cut your losses. But in the question of what to do about an underperformer, ask first whether someone higher up in the organization failed to step up and address performance drift when the problem was much more manageable. The worker in question may be a fantastic resource for you somewhere else. Solve the bigger problem.

Identifying and leveraging underutilized skills is a way to show your commitment and gratitude to your employees. After all, the staffer steps up to perform work that she finds more interesting, and from which she has a better shot at pulling in bonuses and/or promotions. Your organization gains because an engaged, performing employee provides that much more value. The rest of the staff benefits in seeing that you promote from within, giving them reason to work toward advancement.

It's not always obvious when to demote or dismiss an employee. Miscast jobs and systems based on seniority are fertile fields for increasing levels of incompetence. Take these steps to salvage someone you've invested in, but know when you're throwing good money after bad:

- A poor performer often knows when he is being under-utilized or is incapable of meeting the expectations of his job. Work with that staffer's supervisor to identify training and development opportunities to improve performance.

- Failing that, try to train, develop, or coach the worker to meet a different, but comparable, position.

- Try to train, develop, or coach the staffer for a lesser position, one reporting to a different supervisor. When this works, it tends to be because you've reduced the worker's stress, increased his organizational knowledge and support, and removed work they didn't enjoy.

- If this person no longer meets organizational needs, show him out. He may be a better fit in another organization. If you have reached this point, you're dealing with resentment from peers who have had to take up slack, and that's not good for anybody. If the situation is handled early, you'll be in a good position to offer out-placement support, and the former incumbent will have adequate time to begin his job search.

Always involve HR in any terminations or demotions, to save the company and yourself personal liability. Far too often, a remote staffer decides to skirt HR in these matters, and it ends badly for everyone except the lawyers.

Tip 10: Admit hiring mistakes sooner than later

Even after properly defining the position, interviewing the applicant, onboarding and/or using a buddy system, organizations are prone to a common mistake: not admitting hiring mistakes until they're in too deep and have spent more than they needed on pay, benefits, training, and risk.

Why do so many companies wait too long to admit that an employee, even an executive, is a poor fit? It's a particular problem for high-growth companies, which are often in desperate need of staff.

Probationary periods, even best-practice versions of this human capital checkpoint, can miss people who really need to go. Be on the lookout for folks who struggle with low performance, aren't receptive to corrective efforts, and need to step off at the next bus stop. This tough love decision is actually in the employee's best interest. You can improve your overall hiring and training process by learning from hiring mistakes:

- Was the job description poorly crafted or not updated from the past?
- Did someone fail to check references?
- Was a "gut feeling" of bad fit ignored?
- As a favor to the applicant or a third party, did someone set aside hiring policies or procedures?
- What lessons have you drawn from the experience that you can add to your hiring practices?

As in Tip 9, *always* involve HR in terminations or demotions to protect against corporate and personal liability.

Tip 11: Apply Pareto's Law to employee relations
You're well advised to consider the Pareto principle (see Tip 12 in Chapter Tip 5). If you recall:

- 80 percent of your profits (and complaints) come from twenty percent of your customers.
- 80 percent of your profits come from twenty percent of the time you spend.

- 80 percent of your sales come from twenty percent of your products.
- 80 percent of your sales are made by twenty percent of your sales staff.

Pretty handy, right? Here's how it applies to you.

Since Juran first began applying this rule in the 1940s to quality issues, researchers have proved that the causation-effect relationship bears out across a broad range of fields. The break may not always fall 80-20; sometimes it's 90-10, or 75-25 or some such; and sometimes the total isn't 100. But it's still a remarkably powerful observation you can leverage in your organization.

You can save a great deal of money by reviewing your business to find more effective ways to work with staff in this light. You may find that 20 percent of your top performers account for 80 percent of your revenues or profit, suggesting you pay more attention to these stars. Maybe these are the people to whom you give the coveted pay rises or bonus, or send on a critical training course. The important thing is to use the numbers to identify the people who are producing the greatest value, then reward that value.

Manage the Pareto principle carefully. Some employees add value in countless ways beyond direct revenue. These people, through their diligence and expertise, quietly enable the top 20 percent revenue generators to work their magic. Thank these key players (we're not assuming they're the senior management team) and motivate them to stay the course.

Tip 12: Walk the walk and talk the talk

On your quest to uncover hidden millions in your organization, consider Occam's razor: the principle that states the simplest solution is usually best. Because they work, you should use these 12 tips across the board for best results. And that starts with showing your employees that what applies to them, first applies to you.

Be discreet about your finances, spending, and possessions. Be as sensible with funds, even personal funds, as you would have your employees be with the company till. This is the way to build trust, motivation, and partnerships needed to lock down your missing millions.

****

We've just unpacked a lot of insights that are essential to your finding hidden millions in HR. Let's review the 12 secret tips we just discussed to help you motivate your employees in flush times and lean. Then I'll show you how to make the most of this knowledge with the people you support and who support you:

Tip 1: Get the right person for the job

Tip 2: Implement coaching in your organization

Tip 3: Create mentoring and buddy systems

Tip 4: Empower your team

Tip 5: Make the work exciting

Tip 6: Think through pay Raises and Training

Tip 7: Find cost-effective and innovative ways to meet employee needs

Tip 8: Manage expectations effectively

Tip 9: Balance "thank you" and tough love

Tip 10: Admit hiring mistakes sooner than later

Tip 11: Apply Pareto's Law to employee relations

Tip 12: Walk the walk and talk the talk

****

Secret Tips to Better Communicate With the:

Board – Tip 11: Apply Pareto's Law to employee relations

CEO – Tip 2: Implement coaching in your organization

CFO – Tip 6: Think through pay Raises and Training

COO – Tip 10: Admit hiring mistakes sooner than later

CMO/CSO – Tip 9: Balance "thank you" and tough love

CTO/ CIO – Tip 3: Create mentoring and buddy systems

CPO/SVP-HR – Tip 4: Empower your team

Frank Leadership Tips

Tip 1: Get the right person for the job

Tip 5: Make the work exciting

Tip 7: Find cost-effective and innovative ways to meet employee needs

Tip 8: Manage expectations effectively

Tip 12: Walk the walk and talk the talk

Strategic conversations

Whenever HR engages in conversation on strategic issues such as described above, consider that the boss and the boss's boss have these concerns:

I need to know!

I don't know.

Why aren't you telling me?

How can I help you tell me?

Help them fill in the blanks. Help your business sell more, provide higher customer value, attract and retain top talent, account for profits and losses and lead your industry.

Strategy on applying the issues you see through this process

When you see a blind spot opportunity or risk, ask yourself all three of these concerns:

- Do I have the courage to do something about this?
- Do I have the passion to do it even though it is impossible to do?
- Am I willing to share the glory to get this solved?

Coming up: So you think you understand what your CEO and CFO are up to, and how your department fits the plan? Unfortunately, without meaning to, these C-level executives may be hiding millions from themselves, each other, and you. To help uncover that money, let's learn what they know and may not be telling you.

Chapter 8

Understanding Millions in Opportunities: What the CEO and CFO Know and May Not Be Telling You

Of the trillions of dollars flowing around the world every second, precious few find their way to fund our projects. Chief executive and chief finance officers spend a significant amount of time raising money and preparing for the next financing needed. These leaders are so steeped in their expertise that to the degree they think about it, they may assume the rest of the management team understands the fundraising processes as well as they do.

CEOs, CFOs: The rest of the management team doesn't know how to find money as well as you. They need your help. What we're about to get into suggests the sorts of questions your teammates need to ask you in strategic conversations (teammates, pay attention). This primer points the way to cash your business can tap practically without breaking a sweat.

First, non-finance folks, don't worry about the math. We're going to keep this straightforward and relatable, showing you business basics you can build on. Hold on to your seats as we start with the very basics of Fundraising 101 and rapidly move through insider fundraising questions ending with CAPEX and self-funding overviews.

Second, know that you're receiving the benefits of my own education in presenting complex financial ideas that anyone can master. Non-financial types will better understand how to pull in crucial financing when the CEO and CFO do a better job of sharing these secrets.

In this tight lending climate, entrepreneurs of all sizes face starvation. Cash isn't just king, it's emperor—and will remain so for the foreseeable future. Conserving cash offers a clear survival edge, and is hard to pry from people's hands. But even so, you can convince an investor to throw you a lifeline.

Now, let's consider a home-based startup and tend to its care and feeding, learn the basics and move to financing millions.

Why?

Be prepared to answer this numerous times both to yourself, family, coworkers, and potential investors. Call it mission, vision, goal etc. Until you clearly know how to answer to these fundamental questions and can communicate clearly these answers, you may get the wrong answers or results jeopardizing your job, business idea, family life etc.

- Why do you want to do this project?
- What will you give up along the way to accomplish this goal?
- When the time occurs, how willingly will you transfer leadership to someone better suited than you to move to the next level?

Fundraising 101

Credit cards, angel investors, venture capitalists, friends, and family (i.e. rich aunts) are a source for funding for start-up and early stage companies. But what if you can't leverage many—or any—of these? How can you line up the credit you'll need before the bank and other traditional financing sources will take you seriously? The bank wants lots of high quality accounts receivable to loan against, and to see significant investments from the owner, management team, or outside investors.

Good news: the best—and most overlooked—sources of funding may lurk right under your nose. We recommend, from experience, these three top sources for your initial investment. These may not be available for all business situations, but when they are, you have a tremendous opportunity to leverage:

- Customers
- Suppliers/vendors
- Strategic investors

Here's how it works. Let's say you're opening up a restaurant, and you happen to know a wealthy individual who loves dining out, especially at restaurants featuring the sort of cuisine that you specialize in. Approach that **customer** as a relevant investor. Now look at the food **vendors** you'll be supporting over the next year to the tune of hundreds of thousands of dollars in orders. They'll be interested in helping get your business off the ground. Then there's the real estate developer for your building, who has an interest in seeing the property thrive. He might become a **strategic investor** you can count on. In many instances, at least one of these sources might come through for businesses seeking capital, particularly expansion capital. These sources may be able to refer other investors who'll meet future needs. Since capital is fuel for new ventures, think creatively about financing and exploit every good potential source.

As I write this, interest rates are low but many small businesses find themselves shut out of traditional bank lending, as banks are beefing up loan requirements. Financiers usually require you to have already put up your own **capital** as an indication of how much you have at risk should the business fail. If you make a significant personal investment in the business, you're more likely to do everything in your power to make the business succeed.

Financiers come back to what the more experienced bankers call the three C's: character, capacity, and collateral.

Character refers to the quality of your past professional or business relationships, perhaps supported by references, and your potential financier's impression of you: do you seem honest, reliable, alert, and so forth.

Your **capacity** to repay is critical. Here, the financier—whether a it's bank, or an investor, or a trade creditor—will need a financial projection indicating how and when you intend to repay the loan, be it via a series of repayments over a fixed term, or as a total loan return after a defined and agreed period. The bank or creditor will examine the cash flow and repayment schedule. A payment history, both personal and commercial, indicates credit worthiness.

Collateral is security you put up as that thing you pledge to give the creditor should you fail to repay the loan. Whether this is the family home or another property, the lender will need to have a fallback position. You might find additional security in business assets such as inventory and accounts receivable. In the event of a cash flow crisis, you could convert these to cash.

In preparing a credible loan request, take care with your financing application. Haphazard, poorly prepared loan applications strike the wrong impression with bankers and in internal budgeting processes. Woo bankers with accurate, salient numbers: hard numbers about your company's financial performance, and realistic projections about performance. Make a persuasive case for your request, and why the financier will benefit from lending you their money. Above all, document a definite, unassailable plan on repayment.

You can find examples on the Web showing different versions of a one-page summary for a financing request based upon on target audience. Wikipedia offers three versions with its discussion of business plans, contrasting differences in purpose, and target audience http://en.wikipedia.org/wiki/Business_plan. You'll find different sets of key points for executive summaries, covering loan requests, start-ups seeking venture finance, and internal planning.

Microsoft Office, which you probably already have, includes PowerPoint, which includes business plan templates for eleven key issues that you'll need to assemble your summary:

1. Mission statement
2. Team
3. Market summary
4. Opportunities
5. Business concept
6. Competition
7. Goals and objectives
8. Financial plan
9. Resource requirements
10. Risks and rewards
11. Key issues

Omit one of these from your financing summary, and the reader will naturally ask why (unless he simply tosses your proposal in the proverbial round file). Omit *more* than one of these elements and suffer *worse* consequences such as the reader thinking you're clueless about numbers and strategy. There will be no seat at the table for you until you correct that perception.

Reality check: I'm not trying to turn you into an investment banker; rather I'm empowering you to present a winning business request. In turn, the cash you're earning with a sound proposal finances crucial business objectives that you and the rest of the leadership team are going to put to work creating jobs, how'd-we-ever-live-without-you customer value, and a healthy return for your investors.

Still don't have enough capital? Not to worry. You can still start a business by bootstrapping, which we discuss in Chapter 2. For most of us, the first money we get to start a business comes from our partners and ourselves. Either we get along on a shoestring or we mortgage our house. Yes, it's a risk: your risk. You're in business, which means you take risks to follow your dream. Even after you launch, getting adequate capitalization could take years. Meanwhile, you're constantly plowing your profits back into the business. It's how we build for the future.

Know your alternatives

When capital falls far short, and you don't want to bootstrap (again, see Chapter 2), you'll need to turn outside to expand--for funds for equipment and working capital, for example. Then you have two financing alternatives: **debt** financing, in which investors lend your business money, or **equity** financing, in which investors fund all or part of your business in exchange for a percentage of your business.

Learn well these phrases: **personal liability** and **guarantee required**. Pay the loan on time, or your lender has the right to demand immediate repayment of the entire loan amount, and may have the right to seize some or all of your assets and sell them at public auction to satisfy the debt. Non-recourse debt financing requires the assets of the business—not your own assets—to secure the loan.

In **common stock equity** investment transactions, the investor receives a percentage of your business and is normally not entitled to repayment of the principal amount. He is paid when the business has more money though the sale of his stake to a third party or through a liquidity event (normally a sale or merger). This is equity financing; it means that you're selling a share of your business.

Equity financing is a *tremendous* risk. The payoff is hardly certain. That's why these investments are called risk capital. In contrast to lenders, such financiers are legally your business partners, have certain rights to involve themselves in your business, and may even have the right to tell you what to do.

An important distinction: You don't have to repay equity financing as soon as debt; you do repay debt financing before equity under agreed terms. But equity investors don't give you their money without expecting to make a profit, and the riskier the investment, the more they expect in return.

Understand that the odds favor bootstrapping. Everyone talks about getting angel investors or venture capital financing for their special idea. As a rule of thumb, a fund may invest in one in four hundred opportunities presented to it. That is one fourth of one percent. That money comes with substantial influence and controls by the professional investors. Depending upon your area of the country and industry, equity investors often want to see access to at least a billion-dollar market before they get very interested or excited.

For all the reasons in this section, a bootstrapped company, where you have a better chance to control your destiny, may be your best approach.

How to be smart in finding money

When you're building a business, capital inevitably is your chief concern. As stated earlier, few businesses can grow without occasional injections of capital to keep the business afloat, deal with inevitable cash-flow crunches, and invest in facilities, staffing and, new market opportunities. We live in a world of limited financial resources, especially during our riskier, out-of-the-home startup phases. Business owners in need of more money typically furnish it through friends, relatives, and revolving credit.

Bankers want to see at least two years of operations, preferably with profitability before they'll finance, so that's hardly a strong option for most in the early stage of business development. Because friends or family money may be available, and likely doesn't require an application, early stage companies use this funding approach a lot. But remember, losing it can lead to bad blood.

There is a better way. Take the time to find *smart money*. Put the same effort into this as you did in identifying your market.

Smart money provides short-term finance or working capital, which you need to run the business on a day-to-day basis. When we consider interest rate charges, it's more expensive than money that is paid back over a long period, and shouldn't be used for long-term projects.

So where are these investors, already?

Apply the logic that CEOs and CFOs call "follow the money." Research the techniques that raise money in your sector from a variety of investors. Then you'll be prepared when you approach your target investor.

Network, same as you would in marketing. Examine your circle of influence. Whom do you know? Whom have you done business with? Whom did you go to school with? Start there.

Remember the earlier suggestion about suppliers? When suppliers feel comfortable, many will be keen on finding ways to deal with their customers. As a joint venture, both parties have a win-win attitude in negotiations. Do these strange bedfellows sleep well together? Not always, but if they can accept each other's idiosyncrasies they both stand to profit.

Take note of an inherent potential conflict in such a relationship. Although most entrepreneurs want their businesses to survive as long as possible, investors usually cash out after five years. Should entrepreneurs take an investor's offer of cash if it comes with conditions? They may feel pressured to comply, and complying might be the smart thing to do. Not only is the alternative grim, investors can bring more to the table: they often have more industry experience than the entrepreneurs they finance.

Understand your investor

Contrary to popular belief, an investor or even a venture capitalist looking at a business proposal isn't just thinking, "Is this business going to make a lot of money?" The investor is actually wondering whether this business is the best next investment for himself and his funds. Address this question. Establish a business case that wins the investor over. In the United States, we call this the pitch process; you translate your purpose for raising funds into "investorese." There are some essential characteristics of a good pitch:

- Demonstrate a solid, simple **business case**: here's why this is an *exciting opportunity*.

- Demonstrate a **competitive edge** relative to all the other proposals the investor is considering. The competitive edge could be an edge from the product side (fulfilling a need) or from the market side. Then you and your team clearly make competing proposals pale in comparison. Right?

You now have two purposes: one, to get funding; and two, whatever you've set forth in your business mission or vision.

Entrepreneurs and growth businesses want capital, but simply going for the cash without due regard for the investor's strategic interests is a recipe for disaster. Invest the time and talent in forging a perfect fit with a strategic investor. Don't expect investors to jump at your opportunity if you don't convince them that it's in their best interest to do so—beyond all their other potential uses for their money. You'll be disappointed otherwise.

Selling the purpose

Make your business case attractive to the investor, but don't overstate your case. Odds are you're not the next Google, and they know it. If your product or service is genuinely innovative, and offers international applications, don't promise a 10 percent market share of a global market worth $10 billion. You're dead in the water. Rather, demonstrate how you will develop your foothold in that new market, and describe your execution strategy to build from the ground up.

Remember that raising capital is not about finding an investor who's waiting around for you; it's about convincing investors that you, at this time, with this idea, are right for their investment capital. A subtle difference and understanding it could net you millions.

Exploit strategic interest

If you've done your homework, you've found an investor with experience in your industry, or in a complimentary industry. This may yield potential synergies. That is, the investor need not be passive. He or she might bring more to the table than just cash. When Microsoft invested $151 million in Apple in 1997, one synergy it achieved was less risk of adverse litigation regarding its apparent use of Apple-patented intellectual property. Some said this was a hedge against further government lawsuits. Microsoft's Apple investment proves strategic investment from suppliers and vendors even can succeed among apparently bitter rivals—to mutual advantage.

Does this sort of investor need to intrude on your management? It's a double-edged sword. On one side, the input those investors get is negotiable. On the other side, the investor who owns the gold makes the rules.

Here we discuss a pathway to funding: you may need to seek out potential investors where your business will offer an investor a neat, strategic, and potentially synergistic fit to their portfolio of interest or experience. On one hand, we picture the angel investor or the venture capital professional as someone whose only goal is to control the investment—with an iron fist. On the other side, we imagine the investor who is passive and patient. Well, these are generalizations, and not very useful ones at that. Typically, an angel investor takes a minority interest, and doesn't invest more than $250,000 (and often much less). By definition, he exerts little or no control. In most cases, larger investors take a seat at the table via **directorship** or some informal, executive role. Rather than maintain a controlling role, they usually seek to add value.

An individual private investor—particularly one with any amount of considered interest in the business—will be just as valuable. Seek out these folks' participation. Few investors, either individuals or as a VC firm, have any desire to usurp the chief executive or founders, except against the prospect of disorder or financial ruin.

Why you? Why now?

Entrepreneurs of all sizes use business cases to demonstrate to investors that they've got all the bases are covered, and that leadership has a plan to close any gaps and prevent dumb mistakes. If you come to me with a financing request ranging from an early-stage to middle-market company, I'm going to break out the FiscalDoctor's Favorite Top Five Questions for Expansion Thinking:

1. Why should your target customer buy from you, rather than from a competitor?
2. What are the three best products or services we could create in the long term, and how do we best pursue those opportunities?
3. What are the three biggest challenges you face in meeting your budget?
4. What are the top three long-term risks you face, and what have you done to prepare for them?
5. What can we include in this year's budget to minimize our exposure to those risks?

Ask these five simple questions at an offsite location or in a facilitated onsite session, and have someone take notes: you're going to hear an avalanche of blind spots.

CAPEX is your friend

Take note: selling the purpose of investing substantial amounts inside a company is important enough to have its own best practices and procedures. One of the advantages in being part of a middle market or larger company is that

> ### And Then, Sometimes, You Lose
> ### (Just remember to get up again)
>
> What I didn't know could, and did, hurt me. I remember the pain vividly: In November 1987, I was in Houston. After a year of developing a commercial real estate deal valued at more than $100 million, my colleague and I were confident that our buyer, a Hong Kong billionaire, would accept our offer. We were out spending our multi-million-dollar fee. We were on top of the world. However, the day we were to sign the offer sheet was November 19, 1987: Black Monday. Stock markets around the world crashed and burned. Our buyer pulled out.
>
> Of course, he pulled out—he had concluded that new opportunities born of the crash offered greater profit potential than our real estate investment and he rejected the offer sheet, unceremoniously ending my real estate brokerage career.
>
> What could I have done differently? How could I have prepared for this risk? What signs did I miss? None. Nothing would have mattered. This was a tsunami. This was a meteor. This was a historic macroeconomic meltdown. It killed my bourgeoning real estate career, and that was that.
>
> I'm glad.
>
> I wouldn't have thought so at the time, but looking back on what I've built after the fact, in the decades since, I came out of it stronger and wiser, having met and helped people and companies I never would have encountered otherwise.
>
> Try to see your life as one continuous success, no matter the apparent setbacks. Don't be your own biggest blind spot. And enjoy the journey

the divisions often obtain financing through the parent and a dedicated formal capital expenditures (CAPEX) process. Unfortunately, I have seen substantial companies flop at CAPEX, usually because they treat it informally and apply it irregularly. Project results in these cases are haphazard, showing little of the promise carried in the original request. These are the basics of a vigorous CAPEX policy:

- Normally the first part of a CAPEX policy is to state your intent in requesting major financing.
- Next, define progressive levels of authority for the request. This example is named "Levels of Approvals on Capital Expenditure Request Approval"; and it simply shows who has to sign off on increasing requests.

LEVEL	LIMITS ($)	JOINT AUTHORIZATION
A	Up to 5,000	Department Head
B	Up to 50,000	Entity Chief Financial Officer
C	Up to 100,000	Subsidiary President
D	Greater than 200,000	Holding Company President
E	Greater than 500,000	Holding Company Board of Directors

Next a computation method is set out, explaining how the investment payback period or method will be computed, and establishing a threshold projected rate of return that must be met before a project earns consideration.

- A method is normally defined or a group is set up to determine which of the competing projects is to win funding. Few companies can fund all internal requests.
- Now companies learn they can or cannot walk the walk. The process sees a mechanism set up for periodic reports on how well funded projects actually meet representations made to land the funds. Don't accept glib generalizations to excuse underperformance. If your people know they'll be held accountable for representations—in reality, promises they made—then you'll reinforce everyone's sense of fiscal responsibility.
- Part of the best practices for CAPEX policies: a project for reporting overruns. If you catch overruns early

enough, you can prevent them. Skip this step, and your CAPEX policy loses all credibility.

- Did something go wrong? A remediation report assigns accountability to rectify the situation.

- Finally, a completion report compares the proposal to the results, giving you incontrovertible evidence of success and failure. If a power player on your team, perhaps acting out of embarrassment, overrides this tool, your organization could lose millions. Don't stand for it.

If your business is fortunate enough to have grown to the point where you're fielding a significant number of internal financing requests—ideas to innovate, diversify, and modernize—you'll need to define categories for capital expenditure. Now you're allowing different **hurdle rates** within the different categories. Track funding decisions as they support different aspects of your corporate strategy. Examples include environment, health and safety, cost reduction, product quality, and replacements.

Internal funding might be best

By now, you have a sense of how to advocate for your business plan and track internal financing requests. Asking for money is hard unless you're born with the gift; then it's simply a fun contact sport. Just be prepared to spend at least six months on it, from definition of need, to business case, to the money landing in your bank account on a new business request with a new financing source (see below).

When the CEO and CFO—the big guns—go after money, the time required of the entire C-level team is lessened somewhat, but still is significant. Young companies struggle with allocating critical executive attention to the process.

Executives often question whether it really takes "as long as" six months to raise financing. After all, their business idea, company etc., is unique and deserving. Why should it take so

QUESTIONS & ANSWERS

Matthew H. Podowitz |
Principal, Pathfinder Advisors
Atlanta, GA.

Matthew Podowitz is principal at Pathfinder Advisors LLC, a privately held management consultancy, where he helps select clients undertake business process transformations, mergers and acquisitions, restructuring, and turnarounds or post-merger integrations. He also is a volunteer consultant at VolunteerConsultants.org.

Gary Patterson: Matthew, in your experience, where are most organizations overlooking opportunities to save money?

Matthew Podowitz: I've observed that there are millions to be saved or earned within the IT function, which many companies do not pursue or realize. For example:

- *What are you maintaining, and why?* Most enterprises will find money to be saved simply by comparing an inventory of software installed and utilized, which IT can provide, and maintenance payments to vendors, which accounts payable can provide. Most companies are paying support for at least one piece of software they no longer use (or bought but never used). One of my clients discovered he was paying more than $100,000 annually to a vendor for a piece of software the company had retired three years prior, and for which they'd simply failed to cancel the maintenance.

- *Are you overpaying for outsourced IT components?* Most companies outsource one or more components of their IT function, and almost always overpay, not compared to market rate for the services, but compared to what they really need and use. Not every company requires a data center with 99.999 percent availability 24/7/365, but that's what most companies who outsource their data center pay (and overpay) for.

- *Could you save by contracting for IT services on a variable-cost basis?* Many companies contract for information technology services on a fixed-cost basis when they could save money and provide equal support by contracting those services on a variable-cost basis. The outsourced help desk takes an unlimited number of calls each month for some monthly fee. Switching to a cost-per-call basis and taking simple steps to reduce help desk call volume (for example, publish a Frequently Asked Questions document to employees) could reduce the cost of the outsourced help desk by 25 percent or more each year.

- *Use the software you've already paid for.* Virtually every company underutilizes the capabilities of the software they have acquired and implemented, and has the potential to realize significant operational efficiencies and savings simply by better utilizing what they have. The $50,000 document management system already purchased for HR could increase AP efficiency by 30 percent or more if implemented there too. The materials requirements planning system already in use has a forecasting tool that can help reduce materials costs by 10 percent or more by automating vendor price list management, if the company only used it.

- *Put the IT department to work creating business value.*
  The IT department spends some percentage of gross
  revenues every year on maintaining the status quo,
  as that's what executive leadership charged them to
  do. By shifting the IT focus from maintaining the
  status quo to creating value can both reduce the level
  of IT spending overall, and create value elsewhere in
  the business.

*Matthew Podowitz writes several byline articles in industry
journals every year, and is quoted as an expert source on
The Wall Street Journal.com, CIOUpdate.com, CIO Magazine and CIO.com, and WalletPop.com.*

long time to secure funding? Regardless of your proposal, the
process requires you:

- finalize the decision on how much to finance.
- create the business case to support the amount
  to be financed.
- identify the financing sources to engage.
- negotiate the terms of the financing.
- wait while attorneys on both sides finalize the
  negotiations.
- revise the financial projections and business model
  changes numerous times.
- deal with unforeseen crises, absences (vacations,
  illnesses), and everyday business issues.

To reduce that six-month slog for crucial funding, experienced CEOs, CFOs, and/or treasurers consistently invest
time strategically. They obtain **stand-by lines of credit**,
regularly update and inform vendors and banks about the

company's financial situation, and sniff out new sources of financing before the need becomes urgent. Sometimes they even have to play golf with someone with deep pockets. And you thought they were only goofing around on the back nine. No, they're out there working their butts off to raise capital. Improving their slice is only a side benefit.

Chapter review

You need capital to grow your business. Banks might not be your first, or best, source of financing. Ideally, your business may be uniquely positioned to obtain investment capital from customers, suppliers, and strategic partners. Financiers look for the three Cs: character, capacity, and collateral.

There are two alternatives for investment funds: debt and equity. With debt, you agree to repay the loan in a certain period; equity requires you to give up a share of your business. Succumbing to ignorance and fear can result in the piecemeal acquisition of capital, which is not necessarily in the business owner's best interest. Each source of capital must fulfill a particular purpose—say, the provision of working capital, or the acquisition of long-term assets.

The key question for capital providers is whether this business is the best next investment for them and their funds. You must appeal to the investor's strategic interest.

What do you want from someone investing in your business: a passive investor, or a hands-on pro who offers the enterprise complementary skills?

In order to win financing, prove that this is the right time for the investor to commit funds, and demonstrate that your business model is viable and a superior investment compared to other investor opportunities.

In these tough economic times, business owners must match investors' strategic interests. Present a business opportunity that complements the financier's existing businesses by identifying potential synergies. Find likely investors in your circle of influence.

Those who put money into your business eventually will want to cash out, despite *your* being in it for the long haul. Understand money comes with very binding strings. Improvise.

When seeking capital, find the best match with the strategic interests of the investor. In doing so, you'll set up a coveted win-win scenario.

You can follow the money too. Whether you're just starting out in a home, or are a titan of industry valued at billions, these concepts apply to you equally. Just add more zeroes as you grow.

As you grow in size and complexity, what you learned along the way will make you more successful on both external funding or internal funding through CAPEX or internal funding.

****

Bedrock truths:

The Why

Fundraising 101

Know your alternatives

How to be Smart in Finding Money

Purpose of the Investment Money

Exploit strategic interest

Why you? Why now?

CAPEX is your friend

Internal funding might be best

You're on your way to understanding better where to find missing millions. To help finance your great opportunity and exploit those missing millions in finance, Chapter 9 drills down into a dozen secret tips: focused tactics to help you help the CEO and CFO land cash to feed a growing, rewarding business.

Chapter 9

Uncover Extra Millions

Successful leaders raise funds, without which there'd be no business, innovation, or growth. If you're not funding your business this way—the smart way—you're leaving millions on the table for the other guy.

Our story picks up where Chapter 8 left off, drills deeper into planning, and introduces tips to cover fundraising for companies ranging from home-based businesses to blue chip powerhouses. The only difference is in how many zeros you care to add to the end of your financing, revenues, and profits.

These 12 secret tips point the way to financing success for novices and seasoned pros alike.

Tip 1: Write a successful business plan

This is our first tip for a reason. Business plans are key road-map documents that show investors you've assessed your industry, product or service, market, team, operations and financials—and are prepared for risks on all fronts. Business plans help you set targets and measure your success in hitting them. Don't worry, they're not written in stone. But they will help you make a killer first impression.

Typical sections of a business plan include:

Executive summary – This overview of the business plan highlights the most pertinent points from each section. Investors skim this section first. If it fails to impress them, they won't keep reading your plan.

Industry analysis – Shows you know the lay of the land, including opportunities and dangers. Consider supplementing this with a **SWOT analysis** to show you've considered industry strengths and weaknesses your company can capitalize on, and how you'll face challenges.

Product or service description – Now it's personal. How well do you know your product or service? Why is yours a better buy than that of your competitors? Why have you settled on this price structure? If you believe you face little to no competition, say why, and explain why no one else can replicate your model quickly and simply.

Market – Examine your competitors in greater depth. Explain why the market is ripe for your product or service. Here, demonstrate that you have carried out extensive market research and understand how much of your product or service you expect to sell in a given period.

People – You and your team are talented and experienced enough to pull this venture off, right? Prove it. Even if we're blown away by your product, your vision, and your market research, it all means nothing if we don't trust your team. Introduce your main players, and show how their skills and experience apply to this challenge. Why are you the men and women we should trust with our funds? Admit to gaps in your lineup, if any, and tell us how you intend to fill them. Append full resumes for added impact. For a larger company with an internal project, justify why you need the specific high-quality staff that you're requesting for this project.

Operations – Explain how your business will run— which roles do what (and when) in fulfilling your customers' needs. My clients are pushed to include key deliverables by stage or time period to increase the leadership skin in the game to win the race on this project.

Financials – Show your investors that your idea will make them money. In this section, detail your assumptions. Keep them realistic, and demonstrate that your business is sustainable and lucrative. You want to include a **cash flow statement, profit and loss sheet,** and a **balance sheet.** Show the key assumptions crucial to those projections. Business plans traditionally show five years of financials, with profitability or key goals attained within the first 18 months.

Unless you're a very good writer with experience in all of these areas, hire a pro to work with you to make your case. At the very least, have someone who is more experienced than you beat your plan up and tell you where it's weak.

Go into your business plan expecting to unearth opportunities and hazards. Be honest with yourself about what you find, and be honest with your potential investors. If you're just out to misrepresent yourself in a bid to take other people's money, the courts have special designations for that. And this book isn't for you.

Here are key issues professional investors are looking for. This is what you should be prepared to show and discuss:

- **The full financial package:** balance sheet, income statement, and cash flow. Beginners who leave out the income statements and balance sheets aren't fooling anybody. It won't speed up the process, as perhaps they hope to do. It speaks to obvious errors. For example, a preparer who skips the balance sheet likely doesn't see when cash goes negative, when debits and credits fall out of balance, and so forth. I've seen these blunders, and it's never pretty. (You want ample warning before

cash goes negative so you can correct operations before
disaster strikes, as arithmetically it must.)

- **Your three to five key assumptions,** which make or
  break the business model driving your business. For
  example, customer retention rates, the lifeblood of
  low-tech consumer companies and high-tech software
  service models. You need to show you can measure,
  monitor, and master what really matters in your business. When you execute the project, those key assumptions logically flow into a flash report monitoring
  mechanism.

- **Your team's skills and experiences** that make them the
  folks we can all trust to fulfill the mission. Here is where
  strength in each functional area shines. Stress experience
  and skills as CEO and CFO and in sales, marketing, HR
  or the other traditional functions. Plus, acknowledge
  where the team is missing a key skill or individual and
  how you plan to fill that gap.

The goal is for your business plan to be your best friend and
business partner. It wants to do more than just win you internal or external financing. It wants to suggest the path to follow and provide a spotlight to illuminate the dark and scary
parts of the trip, so you attain the goals and vision you set
forth in the plan. Feed it with healthy, accurate numbers.

Tip 2: Bootstrap

Bootstrapping, which we describe in detail in Chapter 2,
is a process of launching your business by spending as little money as possible, relying only on internal resources.
It shows investors you're frugal, smart with resources, and
responsible—all very attractive qualities to numbers people.

Areas where you can spend less and get good value include
Web services and marketing, particularly if you leverage

social media tools such as Facebook, Twitter, and LinkedIn. See Chapter 3 for more guidance on these and similar options.

Companies score funding by keeping costs low at the outset. Learn to do more with less. It'll help you impress backers and land money for growth when you need it. A word of warning: don't skimp on accountancy and legal fees. The truism "you get what you pay for" endures for a reason.

Tip 3: Approach the right investors

Once your business plan is ready—remember, have a pro review it first—present it to the potential investors that your research shows are most interested in your industry, your market and, very likely, your business. Here we consider **venture capitalists** and **angel investors**.

VC's have access to a great deal of pooled money. Tapping one could net you a huge infusion of capital. Angel investors, in contrast, tend to invest their own money, and so tend to have less to give. You might reach more of these folks than a big VC, and they might bring a wealth of expertise you can leverage. On that basis, angel investors may be your best bet.

Target the right investors, not just anyone who will listen to your spiel. Research makes for efficient fundraising. Why are you appealing to *this* investor *now*? Look at what he's invested in recently, and understand why he took that position. Doing so will help you tailor your appeal. Investors also have specific application requirements. Master them. Never give an investor a reason to cast your plan aside on technical grounds.

At the end of the day, if this source of funding doesn't materialize, don't worry. You're in good company. Plenty of businesses balk here and move on with better luck to the next financing methods and strategic partnerships.

Tip 4: Investigate strategic partnerships

"A strategic partnership is a formal alliance between two commercial enterprises, usually formalized by one or more business contracts but falls short of forming a legal partnership or, agency, or corporate affiliate relationship." This definition and a lengthier discussion on this topic and the related theme of strategic alliance are available at Wikipedia url http://en.wikipedia.org/wiki/Strategic_partnership.

From your playbook: "Do this." Finding potential partners takes considerable time and effort, but it can, and often does, pay off handsomely for all concerned. Do your homework. Focus on the target organization's customers, products and services, and business expertise.

Pay attention to the so-called soft aspects of the target organization (and your own), such as company culture, which we discuss in Chapter 6. If your potential partner's approach is to squeeze as much money as it can from its customers, without regard to corporate social responsibility, while you seek to add value to your customers, then this partnership probably wouldn't last.

Structure this partnership so that everybody wins, and the benefits break at 50-50. Document the partnership in such a way that makes explicit everybody's rights and responsibilities. Focus on management experience and marketing. If you can identify gaps in your prospective partner's game plan, that's great: use that information to show how you'll fill in their gaps and describe your contribution here as value you're bringing to the table. (You might walk away with more of the cash you'll generate together, useful if you're seeking to fuel your own growth.)

Tip 5: Build your network before you need it

As you look for funding—well, wait—*before* you look for funding, build and learn to maintain your network. Each of us could do a better job recording business cards of customers, vendors, associates, fellow vets, fellow alumni and old professors, training session buddies, and so forth. Since you last saw them, these folks might have moved up or over into positions from which they can help you. And you might be in a position to help them. It's well worth keeping track of their names and cultivating a healthy network that benefits all concerned. If you only reach out when you're desperate, you'll come off as, well, desperate (and disingenuous). Be yourself. Be sincere. Keep in touch.

Whatever you do, don't rely exclusively on any of these for your network:

- **The company database.** Consider the company database bolted to the floor. You may leave, but it will stay behind, forever more out of reach.
- **Social media.** Do you want to run the risk of having your teenage or college wild night photos attached to your serious request for big money?
- **Wads of business cards** rubber-banded together; miscellaneous index cards. Yes, people of all ages still are entranced with keeping those cards with valuable cryptic notes about where they met, ideas to follow-up or personal tidbits to follow-up. One of the problems is that these cards get lost, smudged, or too numerous to manage. A better solution is look into a contact management system such as the basic one that came with your computer. You'd be surprised how many people simply don't know what software they have on their own machines.

OK, that's all well and good. You'll change the error of your ways. But what if you need help from a network right now? Glad you asked.

There's money close to home: your family and friends, folks who often can help, and really want to see you succeed. Some may charge interest, but if they do, it won't be at bankers' rates. A fast and effective source of funding, this also allows you to sidestep many of the hurdles an institution would throw at you. Sure, your sources will want to understand your plan to repay them, so showing them your business plan will go far.

Now spread out. You also have access to the friends and family of your friends and family, and people you know from other walks of life: neighbors, community members, people who share your hobbies, colleagues, associates in professional organizations, fellow school alumni... Anyone you can reach who would be receptive to your honest message of sharing in the creation of tremendous value. Don't be shy.

Networking is a critical skill for any businessperson, and the Internet has given you tools to succeed at it as never before. Social networking sites by definition provide an excellent medium for identifying and connecting with these people— particularly LinkedIn, a powerful business resource, both to expand your network for targeted companies or skillsets— and to find the people you need to help you grow. You'll find connections across geographic locations, in industry situations, and at companies of every revenue size.

Tip 6: Look into credit union financing

Credit unions now seem to be gaining market share on loans for individuals and small business. And most do not charge banks' $5 to $20 per month service fee. Credit unions, essentially community development financial institutions, are extremely effective sources of financing. In recent years, such institutions have been among the most important for giving smaller amounts of financing to fledgling businesses.

According to The National Credit Union Administration (www.ncua.gov), an independent federal agency, credit unions issued approximately $33 billion in business loans in 2009 alone. That's huge. Some analysts suggest credit unions are gaining in popularity due to their more favorable terms than banks and other financial institutions offer. That is, credit unions may have a greater appetite for risk (see Chapter 1 for more on risk appetite and strategic decision-making). Get in on this funding source, particularly if your credit rating falls below banks' threshold for loans.

Tip 7: Barter for goods and services

Bartering is an ancient and thriving practice in which parties exchange goods and services without using a medium of exchange, i.e., money. It creates value you can put to work. How can you cooperate with a partner on complementary goals?

Let's say you run a popular website. You have advertising slots. Now say you need legal services. Might a lawyer provide legal services in exchange for prominent advertising on your site? Might a gym wanting to advertise on T-shirts provide membership to a quality graphic designer? Might a custodial company clean your accounting offices in exchange for your preparing their taxes? Probably. Keep a receipt.

Tip 8: Consider factoring

Factoring is a specific type of financing where a third party, normally called a factor, loans money to a business based on accounts receivable collateral, normally called invoices.

Although the discount can be substantial, it can help raise needed funds. To get started, contact the International Factoring Association, which provides information, training, purchasing power, and resources for the factoring community.

Here's how factoring works: You sell your accounts receivable to a factoring company, which nets you immediate cash flow for the liquidity you must have. When you invoice, the factoring company collects from either your customer directly, or from you. Should the customer fail to pay, you're still liable for those funds. To take its cut, the factoring company charges varying rates, starting at 1.5 percent of financed receivables.

Consider that the total effective interest rate on factoring often rings in at 30 percent. You might have certain short-term high margin opportunities that would justify that cost. For example, an industry with a very short time from sale to delivering a completed product like the fashion industry traditionally uses factoring. Look to the factoring community for success stories. For example, many young companies selling to Sears are using factoring. Consider this a financial life-support system. When you're ready, move on to less expensive, more conventional accounts receivable and asset based financing alternatives.

There are disadvantages to factoring. Factoring costs add up quickly. As the factoring company takes a percentage of your invoices, your revenues are going to feel the pinch. If your accounts receivable are subject to factoring, you can't leverage them as loan collateral. And should your customers default, you'll still owe the factoring company.

Rather than factoring, consider reducing days sales outstanding (DSO), as this will also open up needed cash flow *without* exposing your business to the added expense and risk of factoring. See Tip 12 for more comments about increasing internal cash flow by reducing day's sales outstanding and other secret tactics.

Tip 9: Find free money

Remember Tip 3, approach the *right* investor? This is that tip's natural complement. Approach the *right* governmental or non-profit organization for money you needn't repay, or for loans offering gentle easier-to-comply with repayment terms for grants and tax credits. How do you see quickly when it makes sense to invest the time and effort to look into either area?

- **Non-Government Organizations (NGO):** such organizations have a tradition of offering money to encourage business to perform some action near and dear to the grantors' hearts. For example, the Gates Foundation encourages help in education and healthcare, and the Kauffman Foundation is devoted to entrepreneurship. Assistance from these and the thousands of smaller non-profits can include money, information, or even moral support. This tip is a sleeper, and it can mean big money for the home-based business and the Fortune 500 Company alike.
- **Governmental:** consider that when state and federal agencies or the foreign equivalents want to help create jobs for their constituents, they offer tax credits. They want to incent you to:
  o Expand jobs in their jurisdiction.
  o Pr ovide workforce training.
  o Move operations into their jurisdiction from another jurisdiction, so that voters in the new state get those jobs.

Traditionally the federal government and military offer a wide range of targeted grants to help finance basic or applied research. Job credits may be the easiest to check into because payroll tax services and CPA firms traditionally keep up with them.

- **Comments that apply to both groups.** NGO and governmental (from either of the two sources) grants are difficult to research because they are available for a rich variety of business purposes, and from a wealth of institutions. As an expert in your particular field, a minimal amount of research and calls to your rolodex should quickly tell you whether this approach might yield money or not.

  Proving your idea can provide the value the grant or tax credit source wants can use parts of the business plan section mentioned above. Although parts of the basic plan are reusable, a business plan for a grant application may differ from the version you show your bank or other investor. Check the grant application for details. Such funders often provide a template for ease and conformity, or you may just have to write something cogent that introduce your business, product, purpose in applying, and explanation of results. Just make sure you're very clear on the awarding organization's requirements before firing off your application. Hire a professional grant writer if no one on your staff has the requisite skills or experience. This is a solid investment on your part. A grant writer is another example of the type of consultant you should get to know, as suggested in Chapter 6.

When considering grant funding, expect that your business will not meet all funders' application guidelines, owing to niche requirements. Fair enough. But ignoring grant opportunities you *do* qualify for is tantamount to leaving money on the table for the other guy.

Tip 10: Work with your suppliers

Suppliers can supply more than they mention on the manifest. They can extend value you can put to work in funding growth right away. For example, ask about extending the amount of time they require you to pay for goods and services to the maximum limit. This creates financing within your organization, and makes good accounting sense. After all, if you pay your bills right away, the money will go to your supplier's bank account, where it will happily nestle and accrue interest. Keep your money in your account for as long as possible.

Tip 11: Learn from mistakes – yours and others'

High school teachers still try to convince us that those who fail to learn from history are doomed to repeat it. As a corollary, insanity might be described as repeating the same actions that have failed consistently and expecting a different answer.

Benefit from the hard-won lessons of my experience:

- Prune your Rolodex every so often to drop the deadwood, but don't abandon contacts just because their contact information isn't current. People move on. You should take the time to find them, and doing so can give you an opening to reach out to them personally. "Sam? I've been trying to track you down since you left WidgetTech! How's your golf game?" It shows you care. These days, everyone's showing up on the Web. Use that resource, and keep your contacts fresh.

- Hire professionals and pay them fairly to incent them to provide value, understanding that this project they are helping with is a non-legal partnership, where both can gain from success. Both parties have responsibilities and accountabilities to each other to attain success. I continue to see and hear about situations where companies have two, three, ten people supposedly looking for financing on a 100 percent contingency payment arrangement. This is almost a guarantee for failure. None of them has enough comfort in the deal to do much more than a token effort.

- Be eager to network and extend favors. The more experience I earn, the more examples I see of karma and the universe providing bluebird opportunities such as an unexpected sale or long forgotten contact turning into a full price sale. One of my stealth projects fell into my lap from an old website, which I barely remembered.

You never know what will result from your doing a good deed, and the benefit may not return to you in a way or from a direction you might expect. But helpful people get help when they need it. Generous people get bailed out. Honest people earn trust and opportunities. It just works that way.

If you feel none of those three lessons applies to you (they do), consider this:

- Which three mistakes did you make last year that you can learn from for success this year?
- Where can this create an opportunity or increase the likelihood of an opportunity occurring?
- Where can you use some information gleaned from last year to reduce the likelihood of a significant risk occurring this year?

Each of these questions, answered honestly, can help you trap and solve a million-dollar blind spot. For a powerhouse checklist on such savings, bookmark resource section seven, which hands you fully a hundred prompts you can use in revealing and conquering blind spots in your life and business.

Tip 12: Self-fund from operations

Now that you have seen how much work is involved in financing, consider diligently self-funding from operations, which is faster. Such funding differs from the CAPEX process discussed in Chapter 8. With CAPEX, the business is the financing source providing funding for your initiative. Think of self-funding as bootstrapping for more mature businesses. Self-funding, in contrast, asks the organization to make much more efficient use of existing operations and working capital.

Here's how to succeed at self-funding:

- **Increase margins.** The longer the time between product and service profitability reviews, the more money, perhaps millions, may be hiding here. Look for where the organization loses money on items sold. Where are you undercharging versus the competition or are providing more than required? Consultants and services are prime candidates of scope creep, which sees them providing extra work beyond that which they agreed to in the proposal, and for no more money. Where should you charge more to earn an adequate return on capital to support the business and research and development? Don't let margins drift downward: keep current on market pricing.
  - o Warning: the lesson of the book is to come together on values, communication, and strategy. When self-funding is considered, it will be key to obtain as much buy-in as possible from sales, marketing, and operations. After addressing valid concerns, move forward understanding that there may still be naysayers who will fight this initiative with a scorched-earth policy. Sales and marketing employees normally lead the opposition, as they believe increasing margins could hurt their sales and commissions. They may

also have allies in other departments who have grown comfortable with customer relationships.

- **Speed up cash collections.** Where can you speed up the billing process by mailing paper and/or electronic invoices and statements more timely, and making regular collection calls? Where can you resolve valid customer complaint sooner?
  - o Not everyone does this basic operational blocking and tackling, though he should. One client's key location decided it was too busy to regularly mail out statements and place collection calls. The result was predictable: cash collections dried up, receivables soared, and proposed bad debts were disavowed as issues "prior people" had created. Restoring normal oversight quickly improved the situation. This isn't rocket science.

- **Reduce inventories.** Create a team to simplify manufacturing, operations, or support to look at product life support issues. Bring manufacturing and support into product design decisions earlier, when costly long-term issues can be identified and corrected.

****

Let's recap. Here are our top 12 secret tips for landing lifesaving funds for your business:

Tip 1: Write a successful business plan

Tip 2: Bootstrap

Tip 3: Approach the right investors

Tip 4: Investigate strategic partnerships

Tip 5: Build your network before you need it

Tip 6: Look into credit union financing

Tip 7:   Barter for goods and services

Tip 8:   Consider factoring

Tip 9:   Find free money

Tip 10: Work with your suppliers

Tip 11: Learn from mistakes – yours and others'

Tip 12: Self-fund from operations

Secret Tips to Better Communicate With the:

Board – Tip 1: Write a successful business plan

CEO – Tip 4: Investigate strategic partnerships

CFO – Tip 2: Bootstrap

COO – Tip 10: Work with your suppliers

CMO/CSO – Tip 9: Find free money

CTO/ CIO – Tip 12: Self-fund from operations

CPO/SVP-HR – Tip 5: Build your network before you need it

Frank Leadership Tips

Tip 3: Approach the right investors

Tip 6: Look into credit union financing

Tip 7: Barter for goods and services

Tip 8: Consider factoring

Tip 11: Learn from mistakes – yours and others'

Strategic conversations

Whenever the CEO or CFO engages on strategic issues, take the time to anticipate that he's in desperate need of your help. Assume he's thinking:

I need to know!

I don't know.

Why aren't you telling me?

How can I help you tell me?

Help him fill in the blanks. Help your business raise that financing to sell more, provide higher customer value, attract and retain top talent, account for profits and losses and lead your industry.

Strategy on applying the issues you see through this process:

When you encounter an opportunity or risk, ask:

Do I have the courage to do something about this?

Do I have the passion to do it even though it is impossible to do?

Am I willing to share the glory to get this solved?

Coming up: You've invested the time and effort to learn more about how marketing, sales, human resources operate and how the fundraising CEO/CFO duo raises money. Put that learning into action: pull it all together and lead the full team to million-dollar savings beyond insurance.

Chapter 10

Make It Real: Your Million Dollar Blind Spots Test

What are you overlooking? What aren't you insisting that your people tell you? How far in the dark are you, and how great is your true potential? Find out. This fiscal fitness health test consists of twenty questions designed to save your business. Use it to move from a scattershot approach to surgical precision inside and outside the enterprise.

1. **Are operations running so smoothly at your company that you consistently sleep well at night?**

"If you can't sleep, then get up and do something instead of lying there and worrying. It's the worry that gets you, not the lack of sleep."

— Dale Carnegie, legendary business author and leadership coach

Our bodies tell us when things aren't going well. Sometimes our bodies know things that our minds don't, at least not fully. If you're not sleeping well, if you're worried, if you're anxious, something might be off at your company. If you're constantly dealing with crises at your company, and have no time to reflect on accomplishments or prepare for the future, it might mean fiscal trouble is on the way—if it isn't at your doorstep already.

2. Are you certain your balance sheet accurately reflects your business?

"Eddie Bauer is a good company with a great brand and a bad balance sheet."

> – *Eddie Bauer President and CEO Neil Fiske...after the company filed for bankruptcy in June 2009*

Since the corporate scandals (accounting and otherwise) of the early years of the 21st century, including the spectacular failures of Enron, Global Crossing, Tyco, and WorldCom, chief executives are now tasked with greater accountability than ever--even personal liability--for certifying their companies' financial performance. If you cannot trust your balance sheet, do you know the right questions to ask to get at the truth? Do you know whom to ask? And do you trust their answers?

A balance sheet reflects your company's fundamental priorities, vision, values, and strategic direction. It's the direction aspect too many leaders neglect. Your balance sheet is a life-saving compass, but only when you have absolute confidence in its numbers, based on a variety of monitors and controls. In what direction is your company headed?

3. Are you satisfied with your capability to project cash availability over the next six months?

Bill Gates supposedly was willing to keep enough cash on hand to pay payroll even if Microsoft didn't get paid for a year.

Cash is king. Cash flow is the lifeblood of business, and is the constant preoccupation of every business manager. Given the recent credit crunch and financial crisis, cash flow is more important than ever. Companies cannot rely as heavily on debt and short-term maneuvers. Know where your cash is coming from.

How much cash must you keep on hand? There's no objectively correct answer. As I tell my consulting clients, the right figure is whatever lets you sleep well at night.

Obviously, every company has multiple constituencies and stakeholders to satisfy. Companies cannot be run solely in the interests of employees, shareholders, vendors, or customers at the expense of all the other groups. You always have to strike a balance. But it is crucial for every company to have a sense of its fundamental goals for available cash.

Available cash reflects how much risk you're willing to stomach, how many months of payroll you want to keep on hand, and, well, what *kind* of company you want to be. Consider three options:

- Stay in constant firefighting mode, even to the extent of funding the next payroll. Don't laugh; IBM felt that pain as a Fortune 500 company before its turnaround.
- Always keep six to 12 months of cash on hand to cover payroll and expenses, as Microsoft purportedly did. This relieves stress on funding, allowing for more conservative management.
- Choose a comfortable option between the two. But let it be your *choice*.

Whatever your answers, you'll have to explain and defend your rationale and strategy in good times and bad. Know your numbers.

4. Are the key facts and measurements you need to run your business and accomplish strategic objectives readily available?

"Measure what is measurable, and make measurable what is not."
— Galileo Galilei

"You are what your record says you are."
                                    – Bill Parcells, NFL coach

If you're a sports fan, you know that sports are measured and analyzed down to every minute detail. Every aspect of a professional football or baseball game is measured, compiled, and correlated. It's easy to tell who won, who lost, and increasingly, why they won or lost. We don't get slow-motion replays in the business world. Although we produce reams of complex data to track our companies' performance, we don't always know which metrics to use. What contributes to profit and loss? Which marketing activities led to that new customer account? Which employees net the greatest gains and losses in the company's performance? The challenge is in knowing which data are important. The ability to measure something doesn't necessarily qualify as a useful metric.

5. Do you operate from at least a three-year strategic plan?

"By failing to prepare, you are preparing to fail."
                                    – Benjamin Franklin

"Planning is bringing the future into the present so that you can do something about it now."
                                    – Alan Lakein, business author
                                    and time management expert

Companies need strategic plans: flexible ones, to be sure, but plans they'll use to guide the enterprise. The sheer act of establishing a clear strategic plan and putting it to work is a sign of fiscal fitness. Companies whose plans light the way at least three years ahead are stronger, sounder, and more confident. They know what they're about, and that's good for business.

In contrast, if you find yourself scrambling at every turn, your plan is pegged to useless numbers, and that's possibly worse than no plan at all. Eventually, you'll sink beneath the waves insisting your compass works just fine.

6. Are you confident that your company will be able to meet your targeted growth in revenues and profits over the next three years?

"The best laid schemes of mice and men go often askew."
                    — Robert Burns, from "To a Mouse"

Companies need to know how to manage expectations for customers, employees, and external shareholders, board members, analysts, and stakeholders. There may be a temptation to under-promise and over-deliver, but that's harder than it sounds when dealing with financial results. Some things lay beyond a company's control. Optimism is a valuable executive trait, but it can blind you to problems:

- What happens if the economy tanks?
- What happens if you lose a major customer?
- What happens if a lower-cost competitor enters the market?
- What else might happen that you haven't thought of or prepared for?

Projections don't exist in a vacuum. A variety of external factors affects your fiscal fitness, many of which you can't control. So try to plan accordingly—not with pessimism or unreasonable optimism, but rather with clear-headed realism grounded in accurate numbers, sound reasoning, and a commitment to your vision.

7. Do your competitors see you as their primary competition?

"I have been up against tough competition all my life. I wouldn't know how to get along without it."

— *Walt Disney*

Who are your chief competitors? Are you sure? Your company might have a list in mind of its top competitors—you know their brands, their customers, and their marketing messages—but what do these competitors think of you? It's possible that your company does not even ping their radar screen.

There are several ways to assess whether perceived competitors truly view you as their competition. For one, are your competitors calling on your existing customers, trying to lure them away? Are you seeing the same companies showing up at trade shows, advertising in the same publications, and targeting the same search keywords for advertising? If you were to ask your customers to list the biggest names in your industry, would you and your competitors appear on that list? Has your company won any awards or honors that your competitors would know about and envy?

If your supposed competitors don't see you as a threat, it may speak to a problem with your company's fiscal health. Our competitors often sense which other companies are healthy and strong. If your competitors don't see you as a force to be reckoned with, able to take away key customers or key employees, you're in trouble.

8. Does your company stack up well against other companies in your industry along fundamental financial

measurements such as gross profit percentage, net profit percentage, cash flow, average days of receivables outstanding, average days of inventory on hand, bad debt loss percentage, and return on equity?

"Tell me thy company, and I'll tell thee what thou art."

— *Miguel de Cervantes Saavedra, from* Don Quixote

Every industry has certain benchmarks for financial performance. It's not always easy to see the whole picture of how your competitors are performing. But by relying on key benchmarks in your industry, you'll gain a sense of your company's fiscal fitness. In the same way, you can ascertain your company's fiscal health in relation to overall industry benchmarks. It's not enough to know that your company earned a five percent profit last quarter; it's better to ask yourself how well you're doing relative to your industry. If your business is a stock or index fund, are you underperforming or outperforming the average results of your peers?

Beware the good times. That's when many companies grow complacent. When your industry is growing fast and all boats are rising, you might overlook weaknesses that explode into problems once the economy inevitably turns south. On the other hand, during a recession, when everyone is retreating and retrenching, even a two percent loss might be cause for celebration and a validation of your strategic plan.

9. Are you in a position to finance growth plans?

"The surest way to establish your credit is to work yourself into the position of not needing any."

— *Maurice Switzer, early twentieth century business author*

How can you finance the fleeting available opportunities to someone with adequate cash available and the ability to make needed leadership decisions? Landing financing is nerve-wracking for many companies, especially in our battered economy. Even well established firms struggle to quickly get credit. Against this backdrop, how might you finance your growth plans?

Politics is often the culprit for this kind of scenario. Companies are frequently reluctant to make a move because of internal constraints that have nothing to do with the operational realities of the business. I have seen it happen with the companies I consult. I am sure you've seen it too. Opportunities get left to languish because leaders are afraid to make some tough choices and ruffle a few feathers. Sometimes the expert from out of town can say what you don't feel comfortable saying. There's an 800-pound gorilla in the room. Someone had better acknowledge it while there's time to save the china.

10. Do you really know your top 10 customers in terms of revenue and total profitability?

"Doesn't anyone here know how to play this game?"

– *Casey Stengel, former manager of the New York Mets, during one of their worst seasons ever*

Your company should make a point of identifying its ten most **profitable** customers. I am continually surprised to learn how often senior executives tell me they don't know theirs. An important distinction: Sometimes companies rate their ten "best" customers according to which customers yield the most revenue. That's one way to measure your customers' impact, but it's not the most useful. The most useful measure of "best" customer is their level of profitability for your business. That is, if a customer brings you $1 million in revenue, of which you only make $10,000 in profit, that customer is not as productive for you as the one who generates $20,000 profit on far less revenue. Sometimes, too, your most profitable customers are the less squeaky wheels who just quietly let you conduct your business. Perhaps you should pay more attention to the less squeaky wheels.

11. Does your management team share and support your corporate vision?

"Leadership is the capacity to translate vision into reality."
– Warren G. Bennis, leadership scholar, author, and consultant

You need everyone on your management team to be rowing in the same direction. Fiscally fit companies tend to have healthy leadership cultures. They enjoy teamwork, and usually live their mission with the good of the whole in mind, not the accolades of the individual. Whatever your vision is for the company—whatever your ideal image of the kind of organization you want to run—ask yourself if your management team understands and supports this vision. If the answer is no, ask yourself how you can help create a more cohesive culture on your management team, or whether there are few laggards or malcontents who need to move on.

12. Are you in a position to seize market opportunities?

"Carpe diem [Seize the day]."

– Horace, Roman poet

"Sometimes the best deals are the ones you do not do."

– Anonymous

There are three ways to examine this question: external position, internal position, and financial position.

- **External position:** how did you find out about this opportunity in the market (whether it is an acquisition, a new technology, or an infrastructure investment)?

Have your competitors already started to pursue similar opportunities, or do you still have the chance to be first to the party?

- **Internal position:** is your company ready to go after a particular opportunity? Is your house in order? Is employee morale high? Are people chomping at the bit to get out there and pursue new business? Does your company have the energy to take on this new challenge of your choosing, or are you treading water? Moreover, ask yourself if you're pursuing this opportunity for the right reasons: is there an organic need for this new opportunity based on where your company stands now, or are you pursuing this opportunity as a defensive move or as a way to keep up with the Joneses?

- **Financial position:** companies need to ask themselves if they have enough cash on hand (or enough financing available) to be able to invest in new opportunities. Do you have enough cash on hand to buy that company, or can you get the financing for the deal? Do you have enough flexibility in your budget to invest in this new IT system, or would you have to go back to the drawing board for the rest of the budget year?

13. Are you pleased with how your customers rate your company's performance?

"Your customers define what you make, how you make it, where you sell it, what you charge, who you hire and even how you fund your business. If your customer base changes over time but you fail to make changes in the rest of your organization, stress and failure will follow."

 – Seth Godin, marketing expert and author, from his blog

Companies should always strive to delight their customers to keep them coming back for more. And it is true that companies should welcome negative customer feedback, as it can, and often does, point out areas for improvement. When the customer cares enough to complain, it shows that he or she is engaged with you, and wants you to succeed. Of course, sometimes the customer is wrong. Maybe he or she simply isn't the right customer for your company. When unhappy, unreasonable customers bog your business down, cut them loose. "Fire" them by no longer doing business with them or send them to a competitor, and focus on the folks who appreciate you.

Question 1 describes the effects of stress you and your people are subject to. Dealing with impossible-to-please customers normally stresses other people and profits. Why not support the common-sense approach: the right customers are more pleasant to deal with and yield more profit.

14. Do your people see you as a successful leader who makes effective decisions, takes decisive actions?

"It's hard to lead a cavalry charge if you think you look funny on a horse."

– Adlai Stevenson

"Leadership is the ability to hide your panic from others."

– Anonymous

Fiscally healthy companies have leaders who win the trust and respect of their teams. Effective leadership can be both a cause and a symptom of fiscal health, but I've come to believe that fiscally healthy companies begin with healthy leadership. It is hard to have a fiscally sound organization if the leadership is lacking.

Often, when companies start to get into fiscal trouble, their leaders reach a critical moment of truth. As profitable and respected as Apple is now, remember the company was an also-ran until they brought Steve Jobs back. Now that it has returned to business leadership, people forget how badly IBM bled buckets of money—suffering a staggering $5 billion loss before Lou Gerstner righted the company.

Decisive, effective leaders don't always make headlines. Some of the best business decisions never get their moment in the sun. They are conceived and carried out behind closed doors by leaders who quietly and effectively steer their companies in the right direction.

15. Does your management team think creatively? Are they "out-of-the-box" thinkers?

"Imagination is more important than knowledge. For knowledge is limited to all we now know and understand, while imagination embraces the entire world, and all there ever will be to know and understand."

– Albert Einstein

Every company, no matter the industry, needs creative people. Companies need creative thinkers to look at problems from new perspectives to synthesize information in new ways, and to produce new solutions and efficiencies. Every time someone on your team comes up with a cost-saving strategy or a way to do more with less, it's an act of creativity. Every time someone in your company devises a new way to harness the talents of your organization, cultivates a profitable new business relationship, or identifies a new strategic direction, it is an act of creativity.

A lot of business leaders think, "I'm not creative." But you need to approach creativity as a broadly defined concept. Creativity is not just about being a performer. It's not just about knowing how to paint or draw or entertain at parties. Creativity also entails the much quieter, more deliberative, behind-the-scenes work that makes up so much of successful business life.

What does all this have to do with fiscal health? Like so much else that I talk about with my clients, the fiscal health of your company is a reflection of the larger picture. If you're a creative organization, where people are encouraged and rewarded for generating new ideas and creative solutions to problems, more often than not, that creativity is going to be rewarded by your customers and reflected in the final tally on the balance sheet.

16. **God forbid, but if you were to get hit by a bus tomorrow, do you have a trusted lieutenant who can step in seamlessly to keep your company on track?**

"Most experts agree that choosing a successor is one of the most important decisions that your CEO and board can make."

— Gary W. Patterson, the FiscalDoctor

Succession planning is not an academic exercise. It's not simply a question of finding the right person. Having a succession plan in place is central to the health of the company. Companies that lack a succession plan are as negligent as parents who lack a will. You need to pass along your knowledge and intentions to guide your company through a transition period and into new leadership—without drama, without infighting, without missing a beat.

17. **Do your vendors see you as a preferred customer, showing how well they value your relationship and business?**

"If you want to be loved, be lovable."

— Ovid, Roman poet

Sometimes a vendor knows more about its customer than that customer knows about himself. When a vendor relies on your company for business, it's a sign they perceive your company as fiscally and culturally healthy. Are your vendors willing to extend you credit, or do they demand to be paid in full, and in advance? Do you get a sense that your vendors are especially eager to work with you, or do you receive indifferent service and have a hard time getting phone calls returned? The former is a welcome indicator; the latter is a canary in a coalmine.

Of course, some vendors are especially hungry for business; others grow complacent with their customer relationships. But in general, by observing the way that your vendors treat you, you'll pick up vital clues about your overall fiscal health.

18. Does your management team feel it receives information about your company and operations in an understandable and timely format to run their departments?

"What we've got here is a failure to communicate."

– from Cool Hand Luke (1967)

"The single biggest problem in communication is the illusion that it has taken place."

– George Bernard Shaw

Communications breakdowns are one of the biggest causes of conflict, organizational miscues, and hurt feelings within a company. Everyone knows that knowledge is power, and at companies large and small, people feel that their leaders are not as forthcoming or transparent as they could be. Consider the examples of sender-receiver blind spots where well-intentioned people in sales, marketing, HR, and the CEO and CFO could improve communications and understanding. Add to that the need for timely, forward-looking management information reports and information to support business teams.

So what's a simple way to gauge how well your business supports management at all levels with usable timely crucial forward looking management information? Just check on the number of days before the board of directors meeting that directors receive the *full* board package. Excellent corporate governance is six days. Longer than that, and information grows stale. Are we talking five, four, three, or two days before the meeting? The day before the meeting? The day of the meeting? That's trouble. The size of this blind spot grows geometrically with time.

Board directors are the most strategic people in the organization. The extent to which they must make decisions based upon poorly prepared information or under fire reflects the size, intensity, and urgency of this silent alarm system. Why? Because if this is how poorly the organization treats its board of directors, how do you think it treats its folks in the field and on the front line?

19. Is your company prepared for changes that a greener economy brings and will require?

We've been hearing about green economy since the 1990s, and it still has passionate advocates and detractors. With implications for issues like health and safety, energy management, buildings and facilities, computing and IT, operations, design, packaging, marketing and end-of-life management, there's a lot at stake—depending on whom you ask.

Where do you stand? Are you practicing corporate environmental sustainability, either out of commitment or under compliance (or both)? The fact is the issue is unavoidable. Whatever your practices, they reflect your values, and they present certain costs and rewards. Think of the goals of a green economy as reducing environmental concerns in a manner that improves both social equity and the bottom line.

Consider energy and your carbon footprint. No matter your industry, you use energy every day, and reducing energy costs adds up to real money. Smart companies look for ways to reduce these costs, and there's no shortage of passion and innovation out there hard at work to make that happen. One of the clearest voices on the planet on this subject is Green-Biz.com. Founded in 2000, it is a leading source for news, opinion, best practices, and other resources on the greening of mainstream business. Check it out.

Should you consider computing your carbon footprint or conducting an energy audit? For example, can you install energy-efficient light bulbs? Can you install energy-efficient windows in your offices? Are your buildings as well insulated as they could be? What if your company could save, say, three percent of expenses on energy each year, especially in a slow economy, when it's tough to raise prices or boost profits? Wouldn't you jump at that opportunity?

Change is underway. Anticipate and manage your part of the green economy.

20. Are you aware of at least one improvement or a change in your company that would significantly enhance your company's performance?

"To see what is in front of one's nose requires a constant struggle."
– George Orwell

Most CEOs are fully aware of initiatives that could yield strong improvements. Yet, for various reasons, the company can't bring itself to change.

Please consider this: these are not normal times in the economy. Every company is under pressure to make a profit and stay competitive, and none of us can afford to keep nurturing "sacred cows" that don't deliver. I challenge you to give yourself permission to make some of these changes that would make a positive difference in your company—even at the risk of political turmoil or short-term pain.

Have the courage of your convictions. If you are like many harried, overworked leaders, your first step should be to stop your analysis paralysis. Put your ideas to work. Learn how to focus on the next steps, and make discipline and drive a normal part of your business life. Finishing one or two projects is more productive than starting a couple dozen projects but letting them slide.

As you reflect on this fiscal fitness test, you'll learn to redefine fiscal awareness, and how to navigate the roadblocks that have kept even consummate professionals from the success they sought way back when they were hungry, lean and determined. You'll attain an inner clarity that will help you meet your personal and professional goals.

You're ready

After reading earlier chapters and taking this fiscal health assessment, you're ready to knock down red-flag moments in your life and business. To harness complete value from this discussion, select three potential topics from notes on either this chapter or earlier that rings true for you, as either an opportunity or a risk. Write down your thoughts on why each subject strikes you as relevant. Trust your insights.

To help exploit that great opportunity and reduce that looming risk in your more focused list of three issues, you need a focused plan your people can unite behind as they add one more task to an already overflowing plate of responsibilities and tactical day-to-day work.

The next chapter will help you triage three topics to help you treat your first focused initiative, and will guide you in tying it all together.

Chapter 11

Tying It All Together

You've heard the saying, "None of us is as smart as all of us." Experience shows it's true. You'll go farther if you ramp up teamwork inside your functional area, throughout your sphere of influence, and across the company as a whole. Help yourself help others. To put this chapter in perspective, consider that there are three key pieces to tie together this process.

- The **POWERS** [2][©] **model** below describes a framework to identify and prioritize where you need to make immediate changes to business as usual. Think of this visualization as the why.

- The **Seven Key Blind Spot Questions**[©] section helps you spotlight and select three key insights you've made in reading this book, or by leveraging the process in this chapter. Think of this as the formula to answer the "what."

- The **Blind Spot Resolution Plan**[©] will increase your effectiveness to apply these insights to your functional area or the business as a whole. Think of this as how to follow through.

Perhaps you're looking for the first time to shed light on blind spots whose disclosure and remediation would make a strategic material difference for the business—that's money back with you, where it belongs. That's risk reduced, eliminated, taught as a lesson learned for a stronger business, a saved career, a rock-solid industry. After you read this chapter, refine your focus and choose one improvement to pursue using the insights you've identified.

The key to your decision is in balancing risk and reward to select the blind spot opportunity. Then pursue that opportunity for greater success, or to take the risk to mitigate either the likelihood of occurrence or the magnitude for the risk if it were to occur. Select the issue that is most appropriate to start with regardless of the functional area it relates to.

Sales, marketing, human capital, finance, and the CEO may even decide the first issue related to another area other than theirs—maybe in IT, operations, manufacturing, and so forth. Every functional area can get a turn as you address the most appropriate issue across the business. You might start with low-hanging fruit, as project managers often recommend. Select your first application in an area to make meaningful, visible improvements you can quickly and easily validate. Once you get some successes under your belt, you'll rapidly debug your process and can move onto more urgent applications.

If you don't have the luxury of time, take a cue from "the burning platform" school of problem solving, which emphasizes immediate and radical change due to dire circumstances. Better to leap from a flame-engulfed oil platform and hope for rescue below than to stay up top and certainly perish in the conflagration. It's a risk, granted, but business is risk.

I normally suggest starting with the low-hanging fruit. You can always start a second, higher-value project after you have gotten far enough on the first project to validate low-hanging fruit results.

Trust in your POWERS^2 ©: the "why" piece of this process

Whether you're new or well-seasoned in issue resolution, I have a best practice model right for you. POWERS^2 is designed to help you identify the problems that keep you from advancing in your career. Use it to advance your leadership skills and boost your earning power. Using it will ensure you select the right problem to solve and you'll know you're not just tackling symptoms. It's strong stuff.

Get ready to harness:

- A clear strategy to remove persistent problems limiting your professional growth
- Insight into achieving your targeted revenue streams
- A practical plan that ensures you'll obtain and sustain all your financial and professional objectives

Supplied in the accompanying graphic is a clear system for visualizing—and concretizing—what otherwise seem like an abstract process. It's called POWERS². The acronym stands for Problem, Overcome, Withdraw, Extract, Review, and Solve & Sustain.

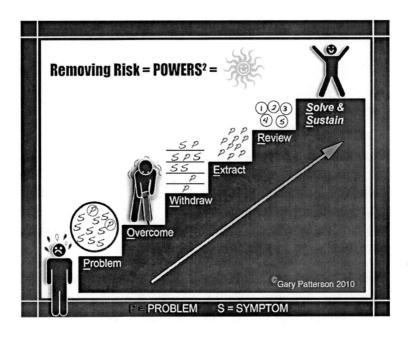

Step 1: "Problem" Start with the stick person at the far left in figure 1.1, whose hair is on fire because he's plagued with issues that seem to block his progress. For example, say he lacks new customers, or has more product or services orders than he can possibly handle. He really doesn't know what his problems are, though he's sure he has some. He's overwhelmed by and is focusing on symptoms instead of his problems. When you're busy or stressed out, imagine the great big ball of issues has hardened a boulder of problems and symptoms. When you *visualize* this boulder you can identify more easily some of the problems packed into it and you're ready to hammer away at the symptoms to winnow out the problems. You can act on problems. Now you're no longer standing there essentially paralyzed, but are prepared to act.

At this first stage, however, you may not even be able to differentiate problems from symptoms. Be patient, we'll get there.

First, here are two definitions to get us on the same page. From Webster's:

- A **problem** is an intricate unsettled question, or a source of perplexity, distress, or vexation.
- A **symptom** is something that indicates the existence of something else.

For example, you may have identified one area of concern: you procrastinate and hesitate to present your ideas at your company. But when you start to burrow into the problem you may discover that what you once thought was a problem is actually a symptom. You may discover that you procrastinate *because* you suffer from stage fright.

Step 2: "Overcome" This step is designed to help you break down your boulder into more manageable pieces and overcome the inertia that prevents reviewing your issues. For some, this may seem nearly impossible as they may feel the boulder has calcified and only a jackhammer can break it. The seven-question process that I will introduce to you later in the chapter will power your jackhammer.

Step 3: "Withdraw" This step enables you to go deeper into your situation and prepare to winnow or isolate problems and symptoms. You begin to break pieces of the boulder so you can withdraw symptoms and problems to review them. Until you look for patterns to suggest underlying problems, the issues all look the same. You should begin to see a pattern in symptoms you're manifesting that keep pointing you to a specific problem. I have found, oddly enough, that many seemingly unrelated symptoms lead us back to one or two big problems.

Step 4: "Extract" After separating your problems from your symptoms, you're in a position to extract the problems, and hone in on them. As mentioned in Step One, in this harried world, it is far too easy to focus attention to solve symptoms instead of underlying problems. Notice that solving a symptom doesn't necessarily solve a problem; solving the right problem solves the symptom. Let's make this crucial step more concrete with an example of a series of questions to sort out symptoms versus problems on the procrastination issue above.

1. Has this been a consistent problem for you?
2. If so, for how long?
3. Under what circumstances do you procrastinate?
4. Do you always procrastinate under these circumstances?
5. Are there times when you have been under these circumstances when you have not procrastinated?

Usually applying a series of questions like these helps identify the problem has a recurring theme. In the example above, the underlying problem this process teased out was a fear of taking a specific action: speaking. After identifying the real problem, you can identify tactics and actions to solve that problem. Resolving the underlying problem gets you back on track to attain your goal. Solving symptoms only leads to frustration because that process may never let you attain your desired result.

Step 5: "Review" At this stage, you should reduce the number of problems into a more manageable list of top priority opportunities and problems. Come up with, say, three to five problems. The goal is to narrow your preliminary list of three to five issues to one initial area you need to work on in order to accomplish your overall goal.

I can't stress enough the importance of limiting the number of problems you need to address. I've seen too many people become overwhelmed after they've identified a litany of problems—they end up doing nothing. When everything is a priority, nothing is prioritized.

Whenever I'm faced with a gargantuan problem, I ask myself, how do you eat an elephant? The answer, of course: one bite at a time.

Now you know exactly what your top opportunity or problem is and you're ready to do the hard work and address it.

Step 6: "Solve & Sustain" At the end of this chapter you'll receive an action plan that'll help you solve your key problem, and obtain and *sustain* success.

Now that you have limbered up your creative muscles, let's use the process shown above with a powerful seven-question process to reach your results.

Seven Key Blind Spot Questions©: the "what" piece of this process

Now that we've introduced the POWERS [2] framework, you're in a good position to answer seven questions that will help you advance your business. See these questions as part of a time continuum that can help provide continued benefits for up to three years. This process draws upon an approach credited to J. Paul Getty, who was, in his time, one of the richest people in the world.

From the current year to year two: unearth and hone in on three immediate problems (see questions 5 and 6 for opportunities), which need your immediate attention.

1. What top three concerns keep you awake at night? Jot down the thoughts that immediately come to mind. Don't spend more than one minute on this question. An example: you do not have enough sales in the pipeline to meet your revenue target this year.

2. What three actions are you willing to take to address these concerns? Two minutes.

From year two and beyond: move you along the continuum to take a longer view of your business and identify problems that you are likely to face down the pike in the second and third years.

3. Which top three long-term concerns keep popping up after you've identified your immediate problems? Jot down the thoughts that immediately come to mind. Again, one minute.

4. Now that you've identified these long-term concerns, what three things are you willing to do to solve them? Again, allow two minutes for potential solutions.

Opportunities that await you: to help you discover the opportunities you envision, *if* you're willing to commit to an action plan that will help you achieve your financial and professional goals.

Now we focus on your future, and the range of opportunities that will result after you've addressed your issues.

5. What are three greatest opportunities for next year that you know aren't adequately funded in this year's plans? For example, securing a new sale at full list price. Take two minutes for upside opportunities.

6. How can you best pursue these opportunities? Again, for the opportunities that you just identified, which three actions are you willing to undertake to put you in a favorable position—allowing you to seize these opportunities? In taking the initiative and drafting the presentation to your leadership team to address an opportunity you see slipping away from a lack of resource allocation. Three minutes for potential answers.

Prioritize your problems and opportunities from the first six questions until you narrow it down to one top problem or opportunity to actually do something about starting immediately.

7. How can you focus with laser-like precision on that issue? You'd be surprised—sometimes solving that one nagging issue can lead you right to the desired opportunity. Now you know exactly what your top issue is, and you've already figured out an action plan to tackle it. Don't stop here. Follow through on your action plan. That's what it's for.

Blind Spot Resolution Plan© (the *how* in this process)

The following eight-point action plan will help you dramatically boost your ease in following through and putting more money in your pocket.

1. What is the first challenge or opportunity you plan to tackle?

2. Why is it important that you address this issue first?

3. What is the first step you need to take to address this issue?

4. What is your time frame for resolving this issue?

5. What is your budget to achieve your goal?

6. Who can assist you and/or hold you accountable for staying on track?

7. What will the outcome or goal look like after you've resolved the issue?

8. What potential benefits in dollars and non-monetary benefits will you realize if you stay committed to the action plan?

The home stretch: your road map to success

Although the action plan is a useful tool in helping you prioritize your problems and decide on a course of action, you need to turn your notes and to-do list into a narrative that you can read today, tomorrow, and for however long it takes you to meet your goal.

To that end, set aside 30 minutes to write a one-page memo that clearly articulates the primary issue you want to solve, the deadlines, and the final desired outcome of your action. The memo should conclude with a visualization of how you look and feel having accomplished your goal.

Note that step eight estimates dollar benefits of this investment decision, the payback component. This can be a sanity check of whether you really should tackle solving this problem. After all, if you don't net enough of a payback from solving the issue, why try to solve it?

When you've completed the writing exercise, I encourage you to make a copy and give it to the person who will help keep you honest and on track. Tack your copy on a bulletin board and commit to reading it daily. Read it aloud until it becomes an integral part of you, your practice, your business success, and your personal record of achievement. You'll have earned it.

Here's to your success and the many opportunities that await you!

If you feel very good about what you have focused on, move forward. Skim the resource section, which has a series of information to help implement your blind spot resolution plan. Execute your plan to resolve a blind spot opportunity or risk to show yourself and others the value of this process. Celebrate and reward yourself. Then return to your notes and solve another issue.

If you want to go the extra mile and stress test the issue selected and blind spot resolution plan, skim or review in detail the next chapter. Then do the same as above. Execute your plan to resolve a blind spot opportunity or risk to show yourself and others the value of this process. *Then* celebrate and reward yourself.

Then return to your notes and solve another issue.

Chapter 12

Bonus Stress Test: Your Blind Spots Solution

By now you've shined a spotlight on a major risk or opportunity, and have your preliminary *Blind Spot Resolution Plan*© front and center. Use this chapter as an optional stress test to learn where you can add to your plan, improving its strategic value.

This stress test methodology serves several purposes beyond testing your preliminary plan from Chapter 11. Use it to dramatically improve the value of any of several key functions, one of which normally exists in almost every business. Specifically, apply this logic in improving some aspect of your strategic planning, budgeting, offsite planning, contingency planning, crisis management, enterprise risk management process, or similar process.

Because practically every company conducts some version of regular strategic planning or updates, the following process offers wide and deep use in improving the results of typical and powerful business function planning.

I've seen this work. I've used it to help companies save millions. When I help companies, we normally attack high-value or strategic blind spots. I wrote this chapter from the perspective of improving your strategic planning process results, so before you read it, view your *Blind Spot Resolution Plan*© as a plan to improve the strategic value of your business.

This process addresses three of the major reasons why strategic planning falls short of its potential at far too many companies, possibly including yours or your partners':

- Inadequate connection to the financial resources needed to achieve the plan
- Inadequate integration with incentive plans, including stock options and equivalents
- Lack of buy-in from participants and employees who execute the plan

Too many companies see their strategies suffer from blue-sky syndrome, which is dreaded almost as much as budgeting. The reason why strategic planning sessions lack credibility among many in corporate America because they're generally seen as detached from the company's bottom-line performance, not because they lack value. That is, the emphasis on strategy is in crafting impressive mission statements, core values, and new initiatives—with scant consideration given to the company's *real* financial position, which is the key to successful strategic plans.

How often have you seen a strategic planning failure because it lacked connection to *reality*—the company's current conditions? I wonder how many companies would admit that in year three, four, and five of a five-year strategic plan, executive teams simply recycle old numbers and hope for the best. More disheartening, far too often, such planning bears little or no connection to management incentives and bonus plans. Sounds simple, but when forced to weigh one decision that helps reach corporate strategic goals against another that increases your personal bonus and that of your immediate boss, which decision normally gets made?

Consultants tend to ask a lot of lofty, bird's eye view questions that don't really get at the heart of the matter. Have you heard these?

- "What adjectives describe your company today?"
- "What adjectives would you like to use to describe your company tomorrow?"
- "If your company could be any animal, what kind would you like it to be?"

Executives leave such sessions scratching their heads. "Well, that was a lot of fun, building castles in the sky; time to get serious. Back to work!" I employ a different approach, and so should you. In my 30 years as a high-growth consultant, I've rescued many a company by pinning real numbers to actual performance. It's real-world, bottom-up strategic planning that works. Here's how:

Bottom-up strategic planning

In this company-saving approach, I ask executive teams to describe their company's bottom line performance based on a review and analysis of financial statements such as balance sheets, budgets, and financial projections. When projections don't feel right I even ask a company to show me its past three years of financial statements. What comes out in comparing a company's spending and budget history to its last few strategic plans is the unvarnished truth (in keeping with the medical metaphor), about its health, its "lifestyle choices," and its life expectancy.

Real numbers, properly analyzed, reveal performance that may vastly differ from how the executive branch *wishes to perceive* the company's performance. While the company's executives can glibly say that business is great, if the numbers show that the company won't reach its financial and budgetary goals, no pie-in-the-sky strategy will help them maintain their competitive advantage. In the end, business is all about cash in the bank, valuable assets, wise investments, a *balanced* balance sheet, realistic budgets and financial projections— and a sound strategy that supports the bottom line.

Fiscal Vision defined

"A strategy without a fiscal vision is like a plane without wings. No matter how hard you try to get your strategy off the ground, it just won't fly."

— *Gary W. Patterson, The FiscalDoctor*

A fiscal vision breathes measurability into your strategic game plan, giving you and your executive team always-on, accurate, and *actionable* intelligence about how your strategic goals are supporting your financial objectives. To this end, I apply the fiscal vision to what, in my experience, are the four most critical drivers of any business: risk, opportunity, change, and uncertainty.

A closer look:

Risk and opportunity focus on the internal forces shaping a company's *gestalt,* that is, its business orientation and management mindset.

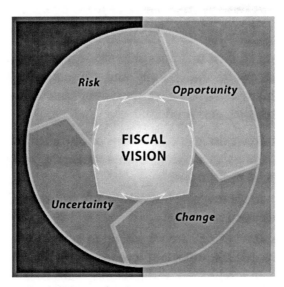

FIGURE 1: Fiscal Vision and Drivers

Change and uncertainty focus on how a company responds or reacts to the external forces (e.g., the economic environment) in which it operates.

Combined, they make up the DNA of modern business.

When executive teams devote an entire session to each driver, using the fiscal lens as their tool, the questions begin to sound like these:

What do the numbers reveal about...

...our attitude toward *risk*? (Session 1)
...our ability to fund new *opportunities*, or unearth hidden opportunities? (Session 2)
...our attitude toward managing *change*? (Session 3)
...our attitude toward operating in an *uncertain* world? (Session 4)

Now let's break these sessions down and harness their power.

Session 1: Risk Driver

"Risk comes from not knowing what you're doing."

— *Warren Buffet*

Management, how well does your strategy support the business risks you're undertaking and contemplating? By the end of this session, you'll learn whether your risk strategy is doable, realistic, and prudent.

- How do we define risk in terms of our historical financial data: balance sheet, income statement, budgets, and financial projections?
- How do we describe our company's culture: risk friendly or risk averse?
- What level of risk are we willing to take for what level of reward? It's important to understand the relationship between level of risk and level of reward as it applies to stakeholders.

- What level of risk is necessary to reach our financial goals in the short term—year one and two—and beyond?

- How much risk can we take on given our company's infrastructure, operations, and management team's mindset?

One useful way to weigh risk and reward is to use a heat map as a frame of reference to prioritize issues. This approach works well in conjunction with the POWERS² process in chapter 11. Let's repeat two of the examples from chapter 1 with the graphic below. A low-dollar issue with a low likelihood of occurrence you might ignore could be lost records or power outage at noncritical facility. A high-dollar value high likelihood of occurrence issue you might decide to prioritize could be credit risk or product obsolescence.

After sorting and prioritizing your business-specific issues with this quadrant, the team has useful information to decide at what point in your processes something must

Risk Exposure Versus Likelihood

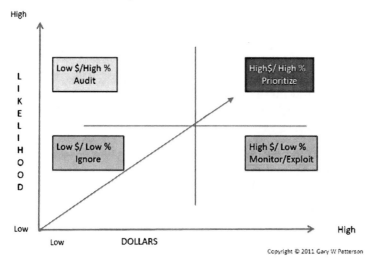

Copyright © 2011 Gary W Patterson

happen, who has responsibility to monitor the issue, and so forth.

Session 2: Opportunity Driver

"Some say opportunity knocks only once. That is not true. Opportunity knocks all the time, but you have to be ready for it. If the chance comes, you must have the equipment to take advantage of it."

— *Louis L'Amour*

It's virtually impossible to consider opportunities without first analyzing revenue and net income, both key baseline figures. Be warned: It's been my experience that far too many financial projections show revenues starting one quarter earlier than will actually occur, and expenses starting one quarter later than will actually occur. That said, brainstorming what opportunities to pursue begins in earnest after management determines and agrees on the company's bottom line. The session starts like this:

- What opportunities do we need to pursue to compete in today's marketplace? Break down the list into two categories: short term (the next year) and longer term (two to three years out). After you've made your list, look at each list vis-à-vis your company's current revenue and net income and projected revenue and net income two to three years down the pike. You're then ready to move on.
- What are we risking to capitalize on short- and long-term opportunities?
- Do these opportunities fit our plans for growth and sustainability?
- What are the gains, risks, and losses in pursuing these opportunities?

- Can we afford to pursue opportunities that knock on the company door?
- What's our cash flow over the next year?
- Is our line of credit adequate to pursue such opportunities?
- What assets can we sell to increase our cash flow?
- What's holding us back?

Session 3: Change Driver

"He who rejects change is the architect of decay. The only human institution which rejects progress is the cemetery."

— *Harold Wilson*

Most companies, whether they admit it or not, know if they are leaders or laggards (and in some cases, has-beens) when it comes to foreseeing and/or adapting to change, especially in these times when "change is the only constant." This brainstorming session requires top management take on its business model to determine its viability and relevance by asking for the participation of each department head. While this may seem like a daunting exercise, you'll be amazed that the smallest financial figure can shine the brightest light. For example, say your accounting department has been warning for some time that certain types of customers, products, or services have been costing the company money. Are you as concerned as they are? Even small losses add up.

Here's a task for each department head: Round up your staff and ask the following questions. Have someone take notes, then sit down and analyze the notes and report on your findings to top management. You'll be a hero.

- What critical factors must we address to prove the viability of our business model?
- What is our department's most pressing concern? (From the basic (maybe our software is outdated),

to the grand (our target audience has changed and
we're ill prepared to connect with our new ideal
customers).

- What resources, including human capital, do we need
  to address these issues?

- What short-term and long-term opportunities must we
  pursue to maintain the department's leadership position (say, three urgent/critical, three simply important,
  and three "if only we could")?

- What short- and long-term risks do we face (from
  "likely to happen immediately," to "will probably happen in the near future," to "it's really too remote to
  worry about")?

- Do our current budget and projections allow us to
  address our most immediate concerns, opportunities,
  and risks?

Session 4: Uncertainty Driver

"Uncertainty will always be part of the taking-charge process."
                                          — *Harold S. Geneen*

The world economy moves at warp speed, giving companies
less time to react to external forces that continuously threaten
their market share and competitive positions: globalization,
climate warming, wars, social unrest, poverty, technological
advances, epidemics, and natural disasters. These forces will
lay their stamp on the performance and bottom lines of your
company.

Industries operate under tremendous pressures beyond their
control, so they're taking risks, knowingly or otherwise, with
every decision made, every action taken or deferred. Reacting
poorly, particularly with outdated or pie-in-the-sky figures,
does irreparable damage to companies large and small, (even
in the best of times, which these aren't).

We don't have to turn the clock too far back to remind our-selves what happens to companies that cut corners, only to see their profits and reputations tank overnight. BP, Toyota, and Bear Sterns are just a few stunning examples of com-panies that bet the ranch and thought they were invincible, or at least disaster-immune. Only after such titans fall from grace do we learn that their strategies and financial goals were nothing more than self-serving roadmaps dictated by man-agement arrogance, greed, and advancement opportunities.

I have found that what's missing in most strategic plans, principally in the failed strategic plans, is the lack of a con-tingency plan, which to me keeps a strategy on the straight and narrow and keeps its management team focused on the well-being of its business. In the end, the utility and effec-tiveness of a fiscal vision strategy lies in developing a contin-gency plan that addresses the scenarios that an organization is likely to encounter over the next three to five years. Unless a management team comes to grips with external forces that threaten to destabilize the company, all the carefully crafted strategies are for naught.

Use this final brainstorming session to focus on developing a companywide contingency plan. The following questions will help fuel a lively, lifesaving discussion:

- What issues, problems, or concerns paint potential doomsday scenarios for our company? Prioritize the sce-narios according to the likelihood that they will occur.
- How prepared are we to deal with catastrophes that are likely to happen? Years ago, Tylenol thought some version of a product issue might occur and had a basic plan to respond in place.
- What safety measures, precautions, and insurance are we taking to prevent catastrophes?

- Can our company withstand a likely catastrophe? British Petroleum still exists. Lehman Brothers does not.

Putting the fiscal vision to work

Today's economy is a perfect storm of rapid change, risk, opportunity, and uncertainty. Executives who come to grips with the financial reality that is driving their organizations' performances and business objectives will be in far better position to lead their industries in new and exciting directions. Of course, embracing such a reality is not for the faint of heart. What is required is the willingness to build—and in some cases rebuild—your strategic plan around a fiscal vision. In the end, a strategy driven by the company's financial performance and goals is a strategy guaranteed to separate the victors from the victims.

You and your management team have a lot to talk about, using this section as a guide. What does your strategy say about your company's commitment to growth, sustainability, and industry leadership? What does it say about you?

Here's to your success and the many opportunities you've created. When you're ready, skim the following resource section, which helps you further identify, discuss, and enact your blind spot resolution plan. Celebrate and reward yourself for a job well done. Then return to your notes and solve another issue. A new day, a new opportunity to do business better.

Resources Table of Contents

Resource 1

Glossary

balance sheet. In essence, a snapshot of a company's financial condition.

balanced scorecard. A single, concise report balancing strategic non-financial performance measures and traditional financial metrics.

board of directors. A body of elected or appointed members who jointly oversee the activities of a company or organization. Also called board of governors, board of managers, board of regents, board of trustees, and board of visitors. It is often simply referred to as "the board."

C-level. Normally reserved for the suite of chief officers, e.g., CEO, CFO, CMO, CSO, COO, and CTO.

CAPEX. For CAPital Expenditures, expenditures creating future benefits.

cash flow statement. Provides three types of information about how cash is captured or used throughout your business for the period measured: operating activities, investing activities, and financing activities.

contact management system (CMS). Think of this as a central database for contact information. Commercial versions normally include features such as: search capability, sales tracking (often with a sales funnel), e-mail integration, scheduling for meetings and phone calls, basic to complex document management, capability to record notes, customizable fields, , and an import/export utility at least to spreadsheets or text.

customer relationship management (CRM). A widely implemented strategy for managing a company's interactions with customers, clients, and sales prospects. Organizes, automates, and synchronizes business processes, principally sales activities, but also those for marketing, customer service, and technical support.

days sales outstanding (DSO). A metric used to quantify the number of days it takes to collect a company's receivables.

enterprise resource planning (ERP). A system that facilitates the flow of information among business functions within the organization, and manages connections to outside stakeholders.

enterprise risk management (ERM). Also described as a risk-based approach to managing an enterprise, integrating concepts of internal control, Sarbanes-Oxley Act, and strategic planning. ERM is evolving to address the needs of various stakeholders at complex organizations who want to understand and manage a broad spectrum of risks.

flash report. Provides upper management with a quick snapshot of priority summarized company performance.

gap analysis. A tool that helps companies compare actual performance with potential performance.

infrastructure. The base of an organization, includes people skills, systems, and facilities.

key metrics. Used to define and monitor critical success factors, preferably in a flash report format.

onboarding, or organizational socialization. Refers to the mechanism through which new employees acquire necessary knowledge, skills, and behaviors to become effective organizational members and insiders. Tactics used in this process include formal meetings, lectures, videos, printed materials, or computer-based orientations to introduce newcomers to their new jobs and organizations.

profit and loss, or income statement. A standard financial document that summarizes a company's revenue and expenses for a specific period, usually one quarter of a fiscal year or the entire fiscal year.

SWOT analysis, or SLOT analysis. A strategic planning method used to evaluate the Strengths, Weaknesses/Limitations, Opportunities, and Threats involved in a project or in a business venture. Normally used in conjunction with revising an organizational strategy or a business model.

Resource 2

Best-Practices Methodology for High-Growth Organizations

Outside service professionals such as lawyers and certified public accountants can be invaluable aides. They alert leaders to risks, opportunities, and rewards worth millions. This **best-practices methodology** helps early-stage and emerging high-growth firms plan milestone moves in leveraging that expertise, which will dramatically accelerate growth.

This is the same resource I provide my clients in helping them prioritize the timing and tasks required to connect with and benefit from such talent, which propels their business or an internal project to the next level. The outline is flexible. I've seen it work at more than 200 companies, including start-ups and emerging early-stage enterprises. The tasks are grouped into two phases: an infrastructure and governance foundation, and then a more sophisticated more mature set of tactics. It'll work for you.

In the first phase...

1. Review audit, law firm, and investor input.
2. Review the business plan to project, in greater detail, what actions are required to meet plan results.
3. Discuss the plan with the functional areas that are responsible for producing these results.

4. Modify the business plan as required.

5. Prepare your action plan follow-up and begin tracking.

6. Review the current system monthly and on an interim basis to increase the quality of the information it provides users.

7. Expand the board of directors reporting package.

8. Identify your needs to select a robust, reliable accounting and back office system.

9. Commit to an accounting/back office system.

10. Negotiate system terms and begin implementation.

11. Expand sales and marketing plans in greater detail and prepare your action plan.

12. Make sure you understand your entrepreneurial company nature, then implement the system and procedure upgrades.

13. Create a staffing plan that covers each of the next twelve months.

14. Estimate the timing of and amount sought for the next financing round.

15. Revise your cash monitoring and projections system.

16. Review the budgeting process.

Thereafter

1. Execute and monitor the items above.

2. Upgrade your human capital capability.

3. Respond to suggestions from your audit firm, law firm, and venture capitalists.

4. Fully implement your system.

5. Adjust to meet key users' new reporting and operational needs.

6. Monitor your business plan, focusing on the category level monthly and more comprehensively by quarter.

7. Continue creating and upgrading systems and procedures.

8. Provide input to raise next round of money.

9. Provide input to negotiate strategic and operational alliances.

10. Create system "hooks" among new back-office system and other information areas.

11. Reassess pricing, commissions, and terms.

12. Review customer support.

13. Mentor the team.

14. Implement the budgeting process, tapping financial statement feedback.

15. Analyze product profitability information.

16. Lead business plan quarterly update.

17. Review continuing professional education policy.

18. Assist on due diligence activities for preparation for acquisition or sale.

Resource 3

Accounting for Success

Once CEOs and their subordinate executives tweak their mission and vision, their next step is to execute their key projects and overall plan. Both preparing to act and acting successfully require extensive input and monitoring from accounting or finance. Know what to expect from your accounting staff.

I'll make it easy. Here's a basic primer on accounting's players and their roles. At the end is a suggestion of when more accounting resources can add value. This is well worth your time as a refresher or, if you're new at this, as an essential guide. Success in business falls to the person who understands the numbers. These professionals do just that. As a bonus, you can use this information in description write-ups for internal documentation and recruiting.

Who does what: Position descriptions

We start by demystifying the function and contribution of the CFO and controller. A CFO is a corporate officer primarily responsible for managing the financial risks of the corporation. They are responsible for financial planning and recordkeeping as well as financial reporting to higher management. This person might be a true business partner or a technician.

Any activity list depends on (a) the size of the organization, (b) whether the organization is public, private, or non-profit, and (c) the industry. The larger the company, the larger the size of the departments the CFO and controller manage. Depending upon whether the organization is public, private, or non-profit, each requires different experiences of both the CFO and the staff. Different industries have their own unique rules, regulations, and attributes, particularly for revenue recognition. One difference is that the CFO in a technology company is more likely to manage HR, facilities, and purchasing than if he were in a non-technology company. A controller is a working manager for the accounting department. This person might be someone on the CFO track, or, again, a technician.

The CFO

Successful CFOs must be jacks-of-all-trades. Generally, they:

1. Are key member of the executive team.
2. Manage accounting and finance functions.
3. Oversee strategic applications of budgeting and planning.
4. Interface with external professionals on insurance, compensation design, and taxes.
5. Liaise with bankers and other financing sources.
6. Suggest optimal financing options.
7. Safeguard assets.
8. Manage information technology in non-technology companies.
9. Upgrade product costing or bidding process.
10. Supervise the controller or accountant(s) and bookkeeper(s).
11. Occasionally manage administrative functions or purchasing.
12. Implement more professional financial and accounting systems.

13. Approve financial statements.
14. Coordinate with external CPA on tax returns, compilations, or audits.
15. Create policies and procedures for implementation.
16. Oversee budgeting process.
17. Create sophisticated cash management.
18. Can sign checks in addition to or instead of the controller or owner.
19. Approve journal entries.

So, those are the duties. When working with a part-time or outsourced CFO, you may wonder when it might be time to take the plunge and *hire this person outright*. Generally, you'll know it's time to hire full-time help when the company grows enough that the amount being spent on the external CPA or part-time CFO suggests this work should be brought back in-house. External equity financing sources often require this position be filled, and may recommend candidates.

Alternately, you may know it's time to hire a CFO when you need to speed up financial statements, require more sophisticated cash flow monitoring, budgets, or variance analysis, when your banker or CPA firm tells you it's time, or when the owner wants to leverage his or her time with a key number-two person.

Resources to tap when hiring finance officers:

The key to hiring this vital team member is creating a job specification to kick off the selection process. Use this opportunity to research what background and experience would help the leadership team meet current and long-term goals and execute strategy. Draft the specifications accordingly and compare candidates to this ideal definition.

Though recruiters (good ones) are adept at positioning you for best-fit hires, which keeps turnover costs down, you might save money (in bootstrapping, for example) by not bringing in a recruiter, but hiring right on your own. Obtain referrals from an existing equity or financing source, CPA, law firm, Financial Executives Institute (FEI), or Financial Executives Networking Group (FENG). If you do opt for a recruiter specializing in executive-level financial positions, you're paying for value in specialized industries, during substantial growth, and when you face major financing needs.

The controller

Controllers also have highly specialized duties that require a variety of multitasking skills. Your needs may vary, particularly in growth situations, but generally, controllers will:

1. Prepare financial statements.
2. Implement basic financial and accounting systems.
3. Implement policies and procedures.
4. Begin safeguarding assets.
5. Create budgets.
6. Coordinate with external CPA on tax returns, compilations, or audits.
7. Create non-standard reports, including variance reviews.
8. Handle insurance and risk management with assistance.
9. Approve customer credit limits.
10. Manage accountant(s) and bookkeeper(s).
11. Handle executive payroll.
12. Sign checks prepared by the bookkeeper.
13. Sign sales tax returns.
14. Create the more difficult journal entries.
15. Process payroll.

As with the CFO, so too with the controller. You might want to bring a temporary or outsourced person in as part of the leadership team. If you're growing such that the amount spent on the external accounting resource suggests this work should be brought back in house, congratulations. Bring this work in-house.

Resources to tap when hiring a controller:

Again, though recruiters (good ones) are adept at positioning you for best-fit hires, which keeps turnover costs down, you might save money (in bootstrapping, for example) by not bringing in a recruiter, but hiring right on your own. Obtain referrals from an existing equity or financing source, CPA, law firm Financial Executives Institute (FEI), or Financial Executives Networking Group (FENG). If you opt for a recruiter specializing in executive-level financial positions, you're paying for value in specialized industries, during substantial growth, and when you face major financing needs.

Here are some other ways you might tell it's time to onboard more accounting resources:

- The company cannot get complete board of director packages to directors at least five days before the meeting.
- Accounting takes more than 15 days after month's end to deliver final financial statements.
- Managers question the value of budgets and budgetary control in running their business.
- Existing variance analysis seems of limited value.
- You need to speed up accounts receivable collections.
- Your banker or CPA firm advises you this position is needed.

Resource 4

Know Your Numbers for Greater Profits

How does your business stack up to these statements?

Here are five of the most common core areas in which we find blind spot opportunities and risks. Improve your information accuracy, and therefore business decisions and profitability, by turning these negatives into positives:

1. My business is unsure who its 10 most profitable customers are.

2. My business occasionally capitalizes expenses that had created an asset with what now may be a questionable recorded value.

3. My business does not know how changes at one of our top 10 customers may affect our bottom line.

4. My business isn't yet looking into an asset that it will be better off selling at a loss to free up cash to pursue a more promising opportunity.

5. My business paints an overly optimistic picture of itself to a customer, vendor, or financing source.

Resource 5

Five Questions to Fuel Expansion Thinking

- Why should our target customer buy from us, rather than from our competition?
- What are the three best new products or services we could create longer term, and how to we best pursue those opportunities?
- What are our three biggest challenges we face in meeting our budget?
- What are the top three longer-term risk area concerns we face, and how would we react if those concerns materialized?
- What can we include in this year's budget to minimize—or eliminate—those risks?

© FiscalDoctor 2012 www.FiscalDoctor.com 678-319-4739

Resource 6

Valuation Basics

Non-financial executives often ask me privately for an overview or simple approach they can use to estimate corporate or project value if strategic objectives are met. Even if you are someone who eyes glaze over when lots of numbers are used, listen up. Understanding this basic financing concept is crucial for you to understand when negotiating to bring in investor capital. Without that investor capital, the business knows it cannot grow and create value for the management team. In the real world, most of these investments fail and most or all the outside investor's money is lost. Hence the investor will only invest when they see the potential to make a lot of money so that they make a series of investments; they earn a risk adjusted return.

I created the example below to influence growth clients to create at least $21 million of revenue in their business unit or company, as that is a point at which more businesses can become interested buyers and are willing to pay a higher multiple than at lower revenue levels.

The table below shows how much those higher multiples can be for the three primary valuation factors used in various industries. For example, if companies in your industry can sell as a multiple of the year five projected revenue, look in the far right column. Year five projected revenues of $21 million valued at a multiple of .75 have a projected value of $15,750,000 versus a projected value of $42,000,000 at a multiple of two.

You may ask why there can be such a large difference in the projected value of the same company when it attains higher revenue levels. The reason is that in most industries, a $21 million company develops a much more robust infrastructure of people, processes, and corporate governance. Then it is easier to implement best practices and attract a larger, often higher quality, customer base than when the company was somewhat smaller at the ten plus million dollar revenue range.

Feel free to add zeros or change the ratios in the table for your particular situation. Please check with your CPA and financial advisor to put this sample to work for your particular situation.

Valuation projections effect factors

Target
Valuation based on year 5 projections of after tax income at various multiples

Year 5 revenues	21,000,000
Year 5 EBITDA	3,780,000
Year 5 after tax net income	3,150,000

Multiple of PE	Projected value	Multiple of EBITDA	Projected value	Multiple of revenues	Projected value
3	9,450,000	4	15,120,000	0.75	15,750,000
4	12,600,000	5	18,900,000	1	21,000,000
5	15,750,000	6	22,680,000	1.5	31,500,000
6	18,900,000	7	26,460,000	2	42,000,000
7	22,050,000	8	30,240,000	2.5	52,500,000
8	25,200,000	9	34,020,000	3	63,000,000

Value does not include distribution of cash and AR less payables
PE does not reflect premium to strategic buyer, who we intend to sell to

Obtain input values from your CPA or banker.

Distribution of proceeds

Non-financial executives also ask me (again, privately) for a simple way to examine the proceeds they may receive after some form of external financing or partnership allocation is satisfied.

The following example below shows potential differences for financing where time or guaranteed multiples are different options offered in the financing discussion, and demonstrates the potential cost of how those forms of financing influences money available to the regular shareholders.

This example is non-industry specific again and projects the company can be sold for $20 million to be divided between the management team and external investors, who provided $3,350,000 of financing to grow the company to the point where the $20 million sale is possible.

Two of the more common ways to earn a profit on the equity they provide is to receive a guaranteed return on their investment that grows over time, or to receive a guaranteed return of a multiple of their investment which does not grow over time. The first section of table 2 below projects how the $3,350,000 grows annually at both an eight and ten percent return. For example, at a ten percent return by the fourth year, the investor receives a priority distribution of $4,904,735 (which includes the original $3,350,000). The second section of table 2 shows results when that investment requires a priority distribution, which does not change over time. For example, the same investment under a guaranteed return of two would earn a priority distribution of $6,700,000 (which includes the original $3,350,000) at the same four-year timeframe.

Whichever of the two return approaches are used, this example assumes that the investor also negotiated a 20 percent override of common stock. That means that after the investor receives the return of their risky capital equity investment and the negotiated additional return, the investor earns a 20 percent allocation of the proceeds allocated to the common shareholders.

The example below shows how the investors receive a total of $7,923,788 out of the $20,000,000 sales proceeds. This means that the management team and employee owners of the company will split $12,076,212. If management members do not go through this basic math and understand where the dollars came in and where they are disbursed before accepting a purchase proposal, you may have some unhappy people. Consider that this can still be a great payout for internal management members if the success would not have been possible without the external investors.

Knowing this math also encourages the internal management team to go above and beyond on executing and creating value to increase the dollars in the sales value to create a bigger pie to divide. Once the original investment and the base return have been earned, a disproportionate allocation of the increased sales proceeds flow to the management team.

Remember that the investor money is normally one hundred percent at risk until the company creates increased value.

Feel free to add zeros or change the ratios in the table for your particular situation. Please check with your CPA to put this sample to work for your particular situation.

Input sectors					Yield recap table - simple annual compounding		
Investment		3,350,000					
Common override		20%					
Sales value at time period selected		20,000,000					

Table recaps showing first dollars to preferred investors at different return rates and time periods — value today

guaranteed return %	1	2	3	4	5	at discount rates
0.08	3,618,000	3,907,440	4,220,035	4,557,638	4,922,249	3,350,000
0.10	3,685,000	4,053,500	4,458,850	4,904,735	5,395,209	3,350,000

guaranteed multiple approach

2	6,700,000	6,700,000	6,700,000	6,700,000	6,700,000
3	10,050,000	10,050,000	10,050,000	10,050,000	10,050,000

An investor gets first dollars as shown above and then share in prorata allocation to common on remaining value.

Proceeds estimate:
Net sales value of	20,000,000	
Less allocated proceeds of (input value from tables above)		
say 10% at end of year 4	4,904,735	*Obtain input
Subtotal available to common	15,095,265	values from your CPA
Additional dollars available to preferred	3,019,053	or banker.
Total proceeds to preferred	7,923,788	

125 Questions to Help You Find Blind Spots

These questions are powerful tools that aid in revealing blind spots—both opportunities and risks—at businesses, non-profits, civic engagement, and even our personal lives. They're the foundation of action plans that produce immediate, dramatic improvement. Think about them. Discuss them with your advisors and partners. Put them to work.

General Orientation

1. What are the top three opportunities or risks we anticipate encountering this year?
2. … And two or more years out?
3. How should we reallocate people, money, or assets to ensure success for an initiative we're counting on for next year's results?
4. What are the three best opportunities we can pursue between three and five years?
5. How quickly can we create a game plan to exploit those opportunities?
6. What are the top three risk areas our business faces in the short term?
7. … And in the longer term?
8. What contingency plan should we create to address the most crucial of the short term and longer-term risks?

9. What are the three most crucial infrastructure issues our company faces over the next three years?

10. What meaningful issue have we put off addressing?

11. Is this issue a chronic symptom, or is it a solvable problem?

12. How can we motivate ourselves and our team to investigate the difference and act on it?

13. Where can we leverage resources toward solving this issue?

14. According to our risk profile, how much time do we have left before this issue reaches critical mass?

15. Who will be blamed if this blind spot becomes visible?

16. What happened at our business the last time this issue surfaced?

17. Why didn't we solve it then, and what did it cost us?

18. What motivates our reluctance to address it?

19. How can we make the shift to see addressing this issue as a benefit?

20. What are the risks and costs of doing nothing?

21. How can addressing this issue *now* unleash additional opportunities?

22. How might better understanding our overall risk exposure and resources actually let us take on more risk?

23. What is my personal exposure in all this?

24. What could we do to supplement or improve our existing enterprise risk management (ERM) program to uncover blind spots?

25. When did we get our most recent external update of our business risk profile?

26. After reviewing my own performance over the past year, where can I commit to working better and smarter in the coming year?

27. What are my top three business strengths and weaknesses?

28. What areas am I willing to work on to improve my performance over the next year—professionally and personally?

29. Are we willing to seek help to uncover our blind spots?

30. Which operations run exceptionally smoothly at my company?

31. How can we build on the strengths of those smoothly running operations?

32. How readily available are the key facts and measurements needed to run our business and accomplish strategic objectives?

33. Do we operate from at least a three-year strategic plan?

34. Am I seen as a successful leader who makes prudent decisions and leads effectively?

35. How do our customers rate the company's performance?

36. How do our vendors rank us as a preferred customer?

37. How do vendors demonstrate their gratitude for our relationship and business?

38. How well does our company leverage opportunities in corporate environmental sustainability?

39. What critical megatrends could create major opportunities or risks?

40. Which single improvement could we execute to significantly boost our company's performance?

41. Which directors' and officers' coverage is available that is not currently included in our insurance policy, which we could adopt to protect board or executive team members from liability?

42. How is our directors' and officers' policy coverage allocated between board and executive team members? How could this leave us personally exposed?

43. When did we last test the adequacy of our media public relations disaster plan?

44. Is our insurance coverage adequate?

45. How long has it been since the organization got an external second opinion of the enterprise risk management program?

46. How much exposure do we have to terrorism and hackers?

47. What are our vulnerabilities stemming from our use of open-source code?

48. How aligned are our executive team and board on our risk appetite?

49. What best practice exists in another division or geographic area, which we could make available elsewhere?

Marketing Orientation

50. How confident are we that our company will meet targeted revenue and profit growth for each of the next three years?

51. Do we really know where, and why, we're making a profit, and where we're losing money?

52. Which products are losing money?

53. Which products should we eliminate (or at the very least raise prices on)?

54. When did we last evaluate unmet customer needs for either product extensions or new products?

55. Which potential product investigations formerly deemed inadequate based on investment requirement, market growth, competitiveness is it now time to reconsider?

56. How strong is our position in seizing market opportunities?

57. Do our competitors see us as their primary competition?

58. Does our entire management team share and support our corporate vision?

59. How long has it been since we last updated our competitive analysis of major business lines?

60. Which new market can we enter with the least risk?

61. Which product prices should we revise upward or downward?

62. Which of our customer-facing activities would benefit from a business process management (BPM) initiative?

63. Where can we improve our use of social media to achieve specific business outcomes?

64. Where can we use marketing and financial resources to exploit a market-offering opening created by a current economic problem?

65. Where can we work with our services group to improve an aging offering's profitability?

Sales Orientation

66. Who are our company's top ten customers in not only revenue, but also in how much they contribute to gross margins and the bottom line?

67. Which are the customer lighthouse accounts (strategic advisors) we need to develop high margin products?

68. Where could unexpected developments, such as a decline in the profitability of our top customers, particularly hurt our company?

69. Where should we change the sales quota structure weightings?

70. Where has our business painted an overly optimistic picture to a customer?

71. How can we provide our sales force with additional training to help them produce more?

72. How could we improve the efficiency of our sales funnel?

73. How long has it been since our last review of key performance indicators (KPIs) for relevance?

74. Which aspects of sales force management automation (SFA) should we implement?

75. Which aspects of customer relationship management (CRM) should we implement?

76. When did sales and marketing last conduct scenario analyses on the various segments of the business?

77. How well can operations handle periodic spikes in capital demand, which sales could create?

78. To what degree are our salespeople merely order-takers, and not excellent salespeople?

79. Where can we facilitate trust among sales and the rest of the organization?

80. How can we better prevent customer attrition?

81. What can we learn and replicate from considering the profile of our three most effective salespeople?

Human Capital Orientation

82. How can our incentive systems better support long-term strategic goals?

83. Which aspects of our corporate culture should we improve for specific gains?

84. Where can we improve our succession plan?

85. Where do we have people struggling in the wrong roles?

86. How creatively does our management team think?

87. Are they resourceful innovators?

88. When did we last examine our staffing levels and staff on a "green field" basis or from scratch?

89. If we were starting a new company today, would we hire the same employees we have now?

90. If we were to hire them, would we want them in the roles they have now?

91. How well do all our department heads show they understand numbers and our business strategy?

92. How well have we conveyed our corporate vision and alignment to employees?

93. How well do employees seem to understand how their efforts help or hinder the company's victory plan?

94. Which areas of expertise are better supported externally, rather than on staff?

95. Where should we increase coaching and mentoring?

96. ... And who would benefit?

97. How could we help our employees become more effective in their first 90 days on the job?

CEO and CFO Orientation

98. How certain are we that our balance sheet accurately reflects our business?

99. How well does our company stack up in our industry according to fundamental financial measurements?

100. Where could we allocate capital more efficiently?

101. How satisfied are we with our capability to project available cash over the next six months?

102. Are we in a position to finance our growth plans?

103. What are the cost of the risks we don't know such as potential inventory mismanagement, hidden product or service quality problems, and inaccurate or unrealistic financial statements?

104. Where can we evaluate and improve the speed and quality of our cash flow and key metrics?

105. What past capitalized expenses that created an asset may now have a suspect recorded value?

106. What asset would we be better off selling at a loss to free up cash to pursue a more promising opportunity?

107. Where has our business painted an overly optimistic picture to a vendor?

108. Where has our business painted an overly optimistic picture to a financing source?

109. How well does our CAPEX system follow up approved projects to learn from investment success and failures?

110. How can we improve our supply chain reliability and effectiveness?

111. How much standby access to financing do we have available for reasonably foreseeable investment needs?

112. What areas of CAPEX should we consider updating?

113. Which of our strategic partnerships would we have been better off not entering into?

114. How could we improve self-funding?

Follow-up

115. Where does our risk versus reward heat map suggest changes are needed?

116. After reviewing this list, what is the first area we plan to address?

117. …Why is it essential we take action there?

118. What is the first step we'll need to take to improve toward that goal?

119. …When will we take that first step?

120. …Whom can we reach out to for help in making that action a success?

121. …When must we have completed this action?

122. …How will we know the process was completed as planned?

123. What potential benefits are we targeting, in dollars and in other benefits?

124. What system can we establish or repair to fully exploit the opportunities that this process offers?

125. What system can we establish or repair to begin to mitigate the risks that this process revealed?

Good work. You can return to this list time and again, and find something in it to trigger dramatic improvement at your company. Copy it out and share it with your team. You never know who'll spot something they can put to work right away, potentially saving you millions.

Your next step is to put these questions to work in building your action plan: to accelerate opportunities and postpone, reduce or evaporate risks large and small. I'll show you how.

Resource 8

Reader's Action Plan

This book, and particularly Chapter 11, is designed to spark creative thinking toward building an action plan, which you can use to reduce risk and dramatically improve your business. Take note of the top three areas of concern you've identified so far and put them through their paces.

Blind Spot Resolution Plan© Notes

First area of concern:

_____

_____

_____

What's the first action you plan to take on this area of concern?

_____

_____

_____

Why is this action important?

_____

_____

_____

When will this first action occur?

_____

_____

_____

Whom can you get to help with the action?

_____

_____

_____

When does the action need to be completed?

_____

_____

_____

How will you know the process was completed as planned?

_____

_____

_____

Which benefits are you targeting (in dollars and other benefits)?

_____

_____

_____

What questions come to mind?

_____

_____

_____

Second Area of Concern:

Now that you have identified a top area of concern, what second area you identified do you want to make partial notes on for follow-up later or a full plan now to put it through the paces?

_____

_____

_____

What's the first action you plan to take on this area of concern?

_____

_____

_____

Why is this action important?

_____

_____

_____

When will this first action occur?

_____

_____

_____

Whom can you get to help with the action?

_____

_____

_____

When does the action need to be completed?

_____

_____

_____

How will you know the process was completed as planned?

_____

_____

_____

What potential benefits are you targeting (in dollars and other benefits)?

_____

_____

_____

What questions come to mind?

_____

_____

_____

Third Area of Concern:
Now that you have identified two areas of concern, what third area you identified do you want to make partial notes

on for follow-up later or a full plan now to put it through
the paces?

_____

_____

_____

What's the first action you plan to take on this area of concern?

_____

_____

_____

Why is this action important?

_____

_____

_____

When will this first action occur?

_____

_____

_____

Whom can you get to help with the action?

_____

_____

_____

When does the action need to be completed?

_____

_____

_____

How will you know the process was completed as planned?

_____

_____

_____

What potential benefits are you targeting (in dollars and other benefits)?

_____

_____

_____

What questions come to mind?

_____

_____

_____

Resource 9

Reader workspace

_____

_____

_____

_____

_____

_____

_____

_____

_____

_____

_____

_____

Resource 10

Do you Have a Question?

I trust by now you're well on your way to managing risk in your operations, avoiding multi-million dollar mistakes, and seizing new and lucrative opportunities to grow your brand, your workforce, and your customer value. As part of your work on Resource 8, the Reader's Action Plan, you might have indicated where you have questions to take your work to the next level. Drop me a line and I'll see if I can get you where you want to be.

Talk to Gary Patterson about your business, and save big: This book covers a lot of ground, and offers in-depth, time-tested advice that leaders at companies of all sizes and industries can put right to work to improve their bottom line, retain valuable customers, inspire employees and live their mission. If you have an issue or challenge you'd like to discuss in detail, or if you'd like to contribute suggestions for another book or service, please visit:

www.fiscaldoctor.com/contact.html

Let me know how you prefer to be contacted.

We update Million Dollar Blind Spots as needed, so keep checking back for more resources. Visit:
www.YourMillionDollarBlindSpots.com

Gary W. Patterson

Understand and uncover your blind spots—and dramatically improve and accelerate your business leadership decisions!

Gary W. Patterson, a 30-year senior management veteran, knows the risks that sink leaders when they're not looking. Whether in sales, marketing, operations, information technology, or human capital, there's something here for anyone in business looking to close the information gap, and impress the boss's boss.

Hailed as a commonsense, value-added approach to risk management, Gary's book helps executives unearth key risk areas and identify opportunities leading to sustainable growth, buzz-worthy customer value, and impressive profitability.

Gary has been interviewed by or presented internationally to publications and groups such as American Management Association, Entrepreneur, The CEO Magazine (AU), Directors & Boards, Risk Management Magazine and More magazine. A KPMG CPA with an MBA from the Stanford Graduate School of Business, Gary has 30 years' experience working with CEOs, board members, executive teams, private equity investors, and entrepreneurs to help them identify and manage the risk factors previously sapping their balance sheets and bottom line.

Avoid costly problems. Increase profits. Uncover your million-dollar blind spots and make better business decisions. Gary W. Patterson shows you how to execute rigorous due diligence and enterprise risk management reviews, and is your partner on your critical fiscal and financial projects.

www.FiscalDocter.com

or Write:

The FiscalDoctor
Gary W. Patterson
812 Hallbrook Lane
Alpharetta, GA 30004

Stick Out Your Balance Sheet and Cough: Best Practices for Long-Term Business Health by Fiscal Communications

How fiscally fit is your company? In *Stick Out Your Balance Sheet and Cough*, Gary W. Patterson shares the proven methods he's developed to successfully treat companies of all sizes, across a range of industries. From a startup purchased by IBM, to a public technology company sold to eBay, to an Inc. 500 consumer goods manufacturer, to an international Fortune 500 firm, Gary's methods flat-out work. Tapping bright, lucid, easily executed tips, tools and resources, you'll give your company an overall checkup to gauge its condition, diagnose problems by reviewing your financials and operations, and implement a treatment plan using best practices from world-class successful companies. At the end of the day you'll own a wellness program tailored to your needs. Master risk, head off increased expenses, close revenue shortfalls, attract and retain the best employees, protect well deserved bonuses, and live your mission. Open this book and say "Profit."

The Fiscal Fitness System: Understanding Balance Sheets, Income Statements, and Cash Flow [Audible Audio Edition] by Made For Success

Accounting is the language of business, but you don't have to be a numbers pro to speak it. Increase your awareness of internal and external forces, figures and functions to excel—even in turbulent times. Harness the fundamentals and put them to work driving decision-making that promotes your wellbeing, customer value and your reputation as an industry leader. Whether you're a first-time small-business owner, are a seasoned pro, or are aspiring to reach new heights at organizations in any sector or of any size, you'll learn how to master financial statements—and meet ever greater goals you'll set for yourself and your organization. Also by Gary W. Patterson: Made For Success Series audio books:

Understanding Balance Sheets with The Fiscal Doctor
http://itunes.apple.com/us/album/understanding-balance
-sheets/id426271703?uo=4

Understanding Cash Flow Statements with The Fiscal Doctor
http://itunes.apple.com/us/album/understanding-cash-flow
-statements/id426272137?uo=4

Understanding Income Statements with The Fiscal Doctor
http://itunes.apple.com/us/album/understanding-income
-statements/id426272606?uo=4

AudioInk Publishing was founded on the principle that "everyone has a story to tell".

"YOU TELL THE STORY, WE TELL THE WORLD"

AudioInk, a division of Made For Success, Inc., is dedicated to providing authors and speakers the opportunity to "Tell their story" through the different mediums available; Key Note Speeches, audiobooks, eBooks and Physical Books, both online and at retail. We provide generous royalties and light costs to authors and speakers in an effort to extend the greatest opportunity to all we have the honor of serving.

There are many ways we can assist you with your project. Please review the list of services that AudioInk Publishing offers and let us know how we can help you.

1. From Manuscript editing to Ghostwriting, we can help you get your manuscript to print. Contact our publishing office at support@AudioInk.com

2. Want a best-seller? Our SnowBall campaign can take you there. Contact our sales office at sales@AudioInk.com

3. Book Trailer videos and author videos: are becoming an integral part of promoting your book and yourself as an author. Want to check out a few? Go to www. AudioInk. com. If you have questions or are ready to get started please contact Bryan at bheathman@AudioInk.com

4. Want to turn your book into an eBook or other book derivative? Contact bheathman@AudioInk.com

5. Once you choose AudioInk Publishing, you become part of a team. Need coaching or consulting? contact bheathman@AudioInk.com

6. Author or Book Website? If you don't promote you, who will? Let us help with a book and/or author website. Contact bheathman@AudioInk.com

You can also Visit our Website: www.AudioInk.com read our testimonials, send us an email, request more information.

Get Quantity Discounts

AudioInk Published Print books are available at quantity discounts for orders of 10 copies or more. Please call us toll free at (888)-884-8365 x 5 or email us at support@AudioInk.com

CPSIA information can be obtained at www.ICGtesting.com
Printed in the USA
LVOW100234111212

311038LV00001B/1/P